D0396589

think
smarter

think
smarter

Critical Thinking to
Improve Problem-Solving and
Decision-Making Skills

Michael Kallet

WILEY

Cover image: ©tumpikuja/iStockphoto
Cover design: Michael J. Freeland

Published by John Wiley & Sons, Inc., Hoboken, New Jersey.
Published simultaneously in Canada.

For general information about our other products and services, please contact our Customer Care Department within the United States at (800) 762-2974, outside the United States at (317) 572-3993 or fax (317) 572-4002.

Wiley publishes in a variety of print and electronic formats and by print-on-demand. Some material included with standard print versions of this book may not be included in e-books or in print-on-demand. If this book refers to media such as a CD or DVD that is not included in the version you purchased, you may download this material at http://book support.wiley.com. For more information about Wiley products, visit www.wiley.com.

Library of Congress Cataloging-in-Publication Data:

Kallet, Mike, 1953-
     Think smarter : critical thinking to improve problem-solving and decision-making skills / Mike Kallet.
          p. cm.
     ISBN 978-1-118-72983-0 (hardback); ISBN 978-1-118-86435-7 (ebk);
ISBN 978-1-118-87125-6 (ebk)
          1. Problem solving.   2. Decision making.   3. Critical thinking.   I. Title.
     HD30.29.K35   2014
     658.4'03—dc23

                                                                                                        2013044790

Printed in the United States of America
10 9 8 7 6 5 4 3 2 1

To my dad, Sidney Kallet, who thought, and thought well.

CONTENTS

Section V

PREFACE

Thinking is the process that every human being uses to solve problems, make decisions, generate new ideas, and be creative. The goal of *Think Smarter* is to answer the question "How exactly do we get better at problem solving, decision making, and creativity?" Actually, the question is "If thinking is what we use to solve problems, then how do we improve our thinking with respect to solving problems?" The inspiration to write this book came from years of helping others answer that question.

People often ask me if it's truly possible to teach people to be smarter. The answer depends on how you define *smarter*. If it means increasing intelligence quotient (IQ) points, then the answer is probably not. But if becoming smarter means applying your IQ in a way that produces more successful problem solving and better decisions, then the answer is absolutely yes.

Critical thinking isn't about making people smarter; it's about using a set of tools and techniques to think in a more effective way. Critical thinking won't increase IQ points, but it will help people apply whatever level of intelligence they have in a way that produces higher-quality solutions. It raises the bar for everyone and improves both individuals' and organizations' overall performance.

Why I Wrote This Book

I had enjoyed a successful career in software development from the beginning of the personal computer (PC) revolution and then worked as an operations and technology executive in the rocketing Internet space. Then, in 2003, I found myself in yet another fast-changing business. I was a senior executive in a telecommunications company, sitting in a boardroom with

20 other executives during the first of a series of strategy sessions to create a five-year plan. A question was raised: What did we want to be five years from then? After a few jokes about running a beach and golf resort in Hawaii, the conversations began to coalesce around becoming a billion-dollar company. A very interesting line graph was drawn. Our revenue had been on the decline; the graph was decreasing through the then-current $400 million per year revenue but then made an abrupt upward slope to $1 billion. There were no discussions about being the best telecommunications company, developing unique solutions, having the fastest network, being the best in customer satisfaction, or being a profitable, great place to work. Rather, we determined that if we were to be a billion-dollar company, we would need to sell so much of this, sell so much of that, and sell it in this number of cities. There weren't any conversations about what we would have to do differently to change from a decreasing revenue stream to a very significant and aggressively growing one.

That was the moment when I sat back in my chair and asked myself a question: "I wonder if anyone in this room, including myself, is actually doing any real thinking?" Soon after that meeting, I started to think about thinking.

After doing a bit of research, I determined that there always seemed to be two ingredients present for successful businesses. The first was *persistence*. Companies that consistently do well embrace a statement I like: "There's always a way." The second ingredient was quality *thinking*: real, hard, roll-up-the-sleeves, not-taking-anything-for-granted thinking. I've noticed throughout my own career that when people really think about something and ask questions—even when they know the answer—they tend to come up with new solutions to a problem, arrive at a new decision, or realize an innovation. It doesn't happen every time, but it happens often enough.

Although persistence is an important ingredient in success, I decided to focus my work primarily on thinking. In the autumn of 2004, I started a company I named HeadScratchers, LLC. The goal was to help people—not just executives, but individuals, supervisors, and managers as well—become better headscratchers, that is, better problem solvers, decision makers, and innovators. I wanted HeadScratchers to take a different approach from the traditional academic focus of logic, inference, and Boolean algebra many other thinking consultants offered. This was about business problem solving, in the real world, for people who needed a few good tools in their toolbox. Our target audience was business people who don't have the time or interest to understand the science of left brain/right brain, neurochemical stuff. The goal was to provide, train, and coach business people with skills they could use, on their own or with others, to be more thoughtful when tackling problems, making decisions, or innovating. This meant training with an interactive workshop, so HeadScratchers became a training, coaching, and interactive workshop company, focused 100 percent on the business use for critical thinking. In 2006, we rolled out our first workshop, "Critical Thinking for Problem Solving and Decision Making."

Whom Is This Book For?

You might be wondering whether this book is worth your time. Consider this: thinking is the foundation of everything we do. Whether you're a novice thinker or an accomplished problem solver and decision maker, is it possible that you might pick up one idea, one technique, or one tool to use in your life—which would potentially lead you to look at an issue, goal, problem, or decision in a different way? If yes, then this book is for you. As a result, you might avoid an error, recognize an opportunity, or accomplish something a little faster or with higher quality.

Why You Should Read a Book Like This

Of course, I am biased and think you should read this book. To be honest, you would get something out of reading any book on problem solving, decision making, and critical thinking. Here's why: when you read a book related to thinking, it will result in your thinking, possibly about what you are reading related to thinking. In doing this, you will most likely pick up at least one thing, one idea, or one exercise you can incorporate in your day-to-day thinking. Your thinking will be different and improved.

So, why this book? *Think Smarter* isn't focused on theory. Rather, it contains real-world tools, techniques, and exercises, which makes a huge difference in your ability to apply what you read. We present numerous pragmatic, straightforward, business-related, implementable ideas with tons of examples. You won't have to translate from a neuroscience discussion to everyday real-world issues.

What should you expect from this book? You'll learn that critical thinking isn't difficult, and you'll learn how and when to apply it. You'll gain many ideas about where to apply critical thinking in your daily job, for both tactical and strategic problems and decisions. You'll obtain tools to add to your existing critical thinking toolbox and will figure out how to think outside the box—and how to get others to do so as well. You'll be able to distinguish automatic from manual thinking and ask questions that generate quality responses.

What I've Learned after Teaching Critical Thinking for Eight Years

- *Everyone can be a critical thinker.* Although some people are more inclined to think critically than others—and although some people become better at it than others—everyone can improve how he or she thinks when tackling problems.

- *We need to be trained.* We all have the ability to think critically, but like many skills, we need to be taught to do it.

- *We forget to think.* We're in automatic mode most of the time and just plain forget to tell ourselves, "Gee, maybe I should think about this a bit." I teach critical thinking for a living, yet even I sometimes forget to use it when it would be helpful.

- *We need to practice.* It's like any new skill; if you don't practice it, you don't get good at it. Practice doesn't have to take long, often just a few minutes while you're conducting your everyday business activities. You just need to remember to do it (see previous bullet).

- *You must have a need to learn this stuff.* It might be based on a desire for self-improvement, more responsibility, or a promotion. You may have a crisis or an elusive goal to achieve. Maybe it's a corporate directive, or you're looking for a breakthrough, looking just to survive, or looking to do something very different. We'll talk more about need later.

How to Read This Book

You don't have to read this book cover to cover, nor completely in sequence. If you already know a little about critical thinking or understand why it's important and what the benefits are, you can start at Chapter 3, "The Framework and Tools." Read that first, before any of the material in the sections for "Clarity," "Conclusions," and "Decisions." After that, you can skip around or read in sequence. In the "Conclusions" section, read Chapter 15, "It's All about the Premise," first, because everything else builds on that.

That's it; have fun.

ACKNOWLEDGMENTS

I'm extraordinarily grateful to my family for countless reasons, and two specifically come to mind with respect to this book. Thank you to my daughters, Rebecca, Jordan, and Julia, who provided a wealth of insights and ideas as I watched them grow up, learn, and apply their thinking. Of course, special thanks to my wife, Stephanie, who for all these years has endured all of my never ending questions—and of course answered the most important question 22 years ago by saying, "Yes."

Thank you to my editor, Stephen Smith, who was able to decipher and translate my brain dumps into readable form with phenomenal turnaround times.

Special thanks to a few of my clients, who over the years continually asked, "Where's the book?"

Finally, thanks to John Wiley & Sons, Inc., for finding and encouraging me to take "write the book" off my to-do list and actually do it. Thanks especially to my development editor, Christine Moore, whose suggestions and encouragement were exemplary.

Section I
Introduction and the Framework for Critical Thinking

This section will introduce a few definitions and terms. We'll cover the meaning of *critical thinking* and discuss what distinguishes it from what we call *automatic thinking*. We'll list many of its benefits and discuss times when you should use critical thinking in your work. Most important, we'll introduce a framework for critical thinking to guide you through the process.

Throughout the book I'll use the term *headscratcher*. You've likely heard the expression "That's a real headscratcher" when referring to a problem to solve, a decision to make, a situation to resolve, a goal to reach, or an objective to obtain—all without a predetermined way to get there.

A *headscratcher* is a:

- problem or issue without a ready solution;
- result or observation without an obvious explanation;
- goal without a clear path.

If you're already familiar with critical thinking, its benefits, and where you can use it, and you have the urge to skip over these chapters, you might want to start at Chapter 3, "The Framework and Tools," where I define the framework; otherwise, start with Chapter 1, "What Is Critical Thinking," where I define *critical thinking*, its benefits, and numerous places in your business you can use it.

1 What Is Critical Thinking?

Thinking is the foundation of everything we do. Every action, every solution, and every decision we make is the result of thinking. We think when we decide what to eat for lunch, how to meet a project schedule, and what to say during a conversation. We think when we drive a car (although, unfortunately, we're not always thinking about driving). We're thinking all the time, and although not always filled with valuable thinking, our brains are always in gear. Even when sleeping, we're thinking.

Critical thinking is thinking but in a different way. Many people describe this process using terms such as *analytical, thoughtful, questioning, probing, nonemotional, organized, innovative, Socratic, logical, methodical, not taking things for granted, examining, details, exhaustive, outside the box, scientific,* and *procedural.* Odds are that you've heard and probably used a few of these terms. But what exactly do they mean?

Some paraphrase critical thinking as "thinking smarter." I paraphrase it as "headscratching." Most would agree critical thinking is not our everyday, automatic, not-really-thinking-about-it thinking.

Critical thinking is:

- manual thinking (not automatic);
- purposeful;
- being aware of the partiality of your thinking;

3

- a process; and

- thinking that uses a tool set.

Here are the details of each of these:

Critical thinking is manual rather than automatic thinking. Let's first take a look at automatic thinking, the kind of thinking we do the most. Have you ever driven your car to work but didn't remember the drive when you got there? How about intending to stop at the grocery store on the way home from work—then realizing as you approached your home that you completely forgot about that errand? What about a time when you put your keys down and had no idea where they went a few minutes later? This is what happens when you're in automatic thinking mode. It is still thinking, but you're not necessarily *aware* of what you are thinking.

Try reading this text:

You mghit tnihk i'ts aaminzg taht you can raed tihs with vrlialuty
no diluftficuy even tuohg the ltetres are mxeid up. It trnus out taht
all you need are the fsrit and lsat leetrts in the crocert pcale.
Tihs is an eaxplme of yuor barin rnuning in aoumtatic mdoe.

How can you read that? When I ask that question, the answer I inevitably get these days is "Because I can read my kid's text messages." Well, that's partially true; but really, how are you able to read that? If English is your native language, you probably even read this as quickly as you would have if the letters were not scrambled.

Your brain does several activities to enable you to read this mixed-up text, one of which is pattern recognition. Your brain is a very powerful pattern recognition machine. You've probably had the experience of talking with someone and being able to predict how they are going to react—because it's a pattern. We recognize many things, such as places, people, noises, and smells. As you start reading the paragraph, your brain automatically starts to unscramble the words—until you get to the word *tuohg*. It's spelled wrong. It is missing a letter and doesn't follow the rule. Your brain recognizes this, so it mentally searches every word you know that looks like *tuohg* and might belong in the sentence. This is called context recognition and refers to what belongs here—what fits based on the sentence's meaning. Our brains are incredibly adept at this. As a result, our pattern recognition, aided by context recognition, enables us to read the preceding passage. However, what if I had asked you to pick the misspelled word? Did you even catch that while you were reading? Most people have a difficult time picking out *tuohg*.

Try this next activity: count the number of Fs in the following paragraph, in 15 seconds or less.

FINISHED FILES ARE THE RE
SULT OF YEARS OF SCIENTI
FIC STUDY COMBINED WITH
THE EXPERIENCE OF YEARS.

How many Fs did you count? Three? Four? Five? We show this in every workshop we conduct, and usually about two-thirds of the class count three, with the remaining counting four, or five, and only a few counting six. There are six Fs in that paragraph, and if you didn't see them all, you missed one or more instances of *OF*.

The Fs test is an example of how your brain discards information when it's operating in automatic mode. Our minds discard things such as this all the time. You throw out some of what your manager tells you; if you are a manager, you throw out some of what your reports tell you. You disregard things your significant other says to you (and get lectured about it later). Why do we throw stuff out? Our brains are bombarded with a tremendous amount of information. When your eyes are open, billions of information bits per second are entering your brain. Your ears are always open, but you block out noise. In an attempt to simplify things for you, your brain throws things out that it doesn't deem important or thinks it already knows. The trouble is that your brain doesn't tell you it is throwing things out; it just does it. Thank you, automatic mode!

Try one more activity: What predominant shape do you see in the diagram that follows?

The square, right? Of course—but it's not really there. Those three-quarter circles define the boundary, but the square isn't there if you move them away. This is an example of how you make stuff up when you operate in automatic mode; that is, you infer things that are not always true.

Your brain's automatic mode is extremely helpful in guiding your thinking. However, unbeknownst to you, it also discards, distorts, and creates information. Although this tendency can be extremely helpful in many situations—such as your drive to work—it can also be a drawback. When you have to think about something important, you want to get out of automatic mode and go into manual—that is, critical thinking.

Critical thinking is purposeful. You make a conscious effort to leave automatic mode as you start to consider a certain situation. You begin to think a little bit differently using some of the techniques of critical thinking. You are very aware about what you are thinking and are thinking purposefully. For example, when you are learning something for the very first time, you are very attentive; you listen carefully to determine whether you understand; you're aware that your goal is to learn something.

Critical thinking means that you're aware of the partiality of your thinking. Most of the people we ask assume critical thinking is nonemotional thinking. That would be great if humans could actually achieve it. But if you are reading this book, you are undoubtedly a human being—and humans have emotions, biases, and prejudices that stem from our values. Although it is possible to be aware of these, it is impossible to ignore them. Your values are a part of you, and as you will read later, play an important role in how you come to conclusions. You cannot be completely impartial, but you can be *aware* of the components of your partiality and how they influence you.

Critical thinking is a process. This process requires that you understand a situation, come to a conclusion about what to do, and take action on that conclusion. We have many processes in business—the steps we follow to get us from A to B. For example, a customer who has a problem may call customer care. A typical process there might include understanding why the customer is calling, assessing the situation, asking a series of questions, perhaps looking information up in a database, and coming to conclusions about what the issue is, what you can do about it, or whether you have to escalate it.

Critical thinking is conducted within a framework and tool set. The framework consists of a three-step process. The tool set consists of the individual critical thinking techniques used in each step to guide your manual thinking.

Benefits of Critical Thinking

Critical thinking can significantly enhance your problem-solving and decision-making skills. You make better-quality decisions, come up with more innovative solutions, and enjoy faster outcomes. Some benefits of critical thinking include:

- clear understanding of problems or situations
- faster and accurate conclusions and quality decisions
- a richer variety of explanations and solutions
- opportunity recognition
- mistake avoidance
- thought-out strategies and early elimination of dead ends

Critical thinking achieves these benefits by affecting three main aspects of your thought process, explained next.

Critical Thinking Enables You to Look at Issues Differently

We often look at the problems we have to solve from a certain perspective. This means that you get a set of solutions that are consistent with the way you interpret the problem. However, when you use critical thinking tools to review problems differently, you get new perspectives and ideas.

For example, suppose your shoelace broke on your tennis shoe. If your goal was simply to fix it quickly, you might just tie the dislodged piece with a knot to the rest of the lace and jury-rig the tennis shoe tight. But if you wanted to fix it so it would last, you might replace the shoelace with another. If you decide the shoes are old and uncomfortable, you might buy another pair.

In business, you might receive customer calls about lowering the fee for service. From the perspective of keeping the customers at all costs, you might give them a discount. If your goal above all else is to provide a fair price for the value, you might have a conversation with them about the value of your service and not give them a discount, with the understanding they might not renew.

Suppose there was a spike in the workload of your department. If you thought the workload change was only temporary, you might ask your folks to work overtime or perhaps hire a short-term contractor. But if you thought the workload increase was permanent, you might start interviewing for a new full-time hire.

As you can see, different perspectives result in different solutions.

Critical Thinking Prevents a Distorted Picture

You saw in the examples at the beginning of the chapter how your brain hides information, imagines, and throws things out when operating in automatic mode. Interpretations of statements and situations vary greatly as your automatic brain attempts to compare them to a prior known situation. For example, you might misinterpret a request from a customer because you automatically think it is the same as others you recently fulfilled. Issues you think are clear are not always actually clear. Critical thinking, and being conscious about what you are thinking, minimizes this distortion and allows you to examine a situation anew.

How often are you asked for something that you respond to automatically using solely your prior experience? Without looking more clearly, you might not recognize the situation at hand is actually a bit different from prior situations—and this time, the answer can be different as well. For example, if you had a job in accounts payable, you would be accustomed to many calls from your suppliers asking for expedited payment of their invoices. When you receive your next request for faster payment, you might automatically say, "I'm sorry, we cannot. Our company policy is to pay in 45 days." However, perhaps your supplier actually sent in the invoice more than four months prior, and it was misplaced within your company. Knowing this, you would have responded, "I'm sorry, we'll expedite payment of the invoice, and you'll have payment in five days."

Critical Thinking Gives You a Framework to Think In

A framework to think in provides two huge benefits: it helps organize and guide your thinking while leveraging and incorporating others' input as well.

- *Organizing your thoughts:* Many of us think in a somewhat haphazard manner, causing us to rethink the same issue and to forget what we have already figured out, assumed, or even decided. Critical thinking helps sort it all out.

- *Incorporating others' thinking:* An important part of the critical thinking process is listening to others explain *their* thinking—which allows two things to occur. First, you might realize that others have ideas to help solve your problem. After all, you don't have exclusivity on all the good ideas. Second, listening to others' thinking stimulates new thinking in you. As a result, you may come up with ideas you would have never thought about had you not had that interaction.

The Takeaway

Critical thinking is a purposeful method for *enhancing your thoughts beyond your automatic, everyday way of thinking. It's a process that uses a framework and tool set.* The benefits result from changing the way you look at issues, organizing your thoughts, and incorporating others' thoughts. It stimulates new perspectives and prevents distorted views of a situation. As a result, your problem-solving and decision-making skills are enhanced.

2 When to Use Critical Thinking

The previous chapter outlined some of the benefits of critical thinking. With so many advantages, it would seem we should think critically all the time. Although critical thinking is always useful and can be applied everywhere, it's not practical to think this way all the time. It's not only about where you apply critical thinking but also about when you apply it.

A simple rule to determine whether you should employ critical thinking in a given situation is when the result of a problem, initiative, goal, or circumstance (a headscratcher) is substantial. In other words, use critical thinking when the outcome makes a significant difference in your business or personal situation.

For example, a casual e-mail about where to eat lunch usually isn't catastrophic if there's a miscommunication. However, a misunderstood e-mail about the requirements of a product, or about a customer issue, may have far-reaching ramifications. As a result, you might want to use a little critical thinking on the e-mail that describes a customer issue, as opposed to the e-mail about lunch.

The following are three lists of examples of where and when you might use critical thinking. The first list contains high-level business functions; the second, specific business issues or goals; and the third, day-to-day activities many use to achieve those business goals. Once you learn the critical thinking tools, you'll add to this list with areas specific to your job.

List 1: Business Functions That Benefit from Critical Thinking

- Account management
- Automation
- Budgeting
- Build versus buy decisions
- Competitive analysis
- Contracts
- Cost-reduction initiatives
- Crisis management
- Customer care improvement
- Customer retention strategies
- Development processes
- Diagnosis
- Employee leadership development
- Employee productivity
- Financial decisions
- Human resources issues
- Information systems
- Inventory control
- Investment management
- Mergers and acquisitions
- New product ideas and creation
- Operational efficiency
- Outsource versus in-source decisions
- Partnership-related issues
- Product management
- Product marketing

- Project management
- Proposal evaluations
- Quality assurance control
- Resource management
- Responses to requests for information (RFIs), requests for proposals (RFPs), and bids
- Revenue generation strategies
- Risk management
- Sales and marketing tactics
- Short- and long-term business strategies
- Space planning
- Succession planning
- Task coordination
- Technology infrastructure
- Time, cost, and resource planning

List 2: Examples of Specific Business Issues and Goals for Which Critical Thinking Should Be Used

To understand a situation that is unclear:

- There is a flurry of activity in sales and the pipeline is at high levels, yet closed sales are flat.
- Customer care call volume has significantly changed for no apparent reason.
- A series of manufacturing errors has occurred without an explanation.
- Prospective customers *seem* interested in your product, yet few actually buy it.
- The cost of operations is increasing, but the volumes being processed are not.

- A project plan has milestones with particular dates and deliverables, but people aren't meeting the time-frame deadlines.

- A change in the norm has occurred with no obvious explanation.

- The metrics you're tracking are not capable of guiding improvement or predicting an outcome.

- You've made a call for root-cause analysis to find the original cause of something, and it produces an unexpected result.

- Inventory or usage of parts does not reconcile with the finished product.

- Delivered products or services do not reconcile with bills or revenue.

- Incremental expenses in growth do not equal decremental savings in reduction.

- Two people using the same data obtain different conclusions.

- Conclusions about data don't add up or make sense.

- The graph of something measured or projected has a sudden slope change.

- Customers are reporting an error rate that is significantly different from what you are measuring.

To improve something:

- To decrease the cost of customer care by 25 percent yet increase customer satisfaction.

- To increase productivity.

- To improve communications between your department and another.

- To determine how to change the marketing strategy to be more competitive.

- To grow your business.

- To decrease costs by 25 percent.

- To find and hire more qualified candidates.

- To determine what to do with ever-increasing health care costs.

- To shorten development times by a third.

- To decrease mean time to repair (MTR) by 20 percent.

- To shorten order-to-delivery time by half.

- To increase the quality of products so that the customer rating is 5 out of 5.

- To improve an advertising campaign's results.

When looking toward the future, consider:

- How can we create a new product that will compete with the new service our primary competitor just introduced?

- Two key employees just quit—now what?

- Our legacy product, which produces the majority of our revenues and profit, has a high attrition rate. What should we do?

- How do we avoid *this* [insert unpleasant event] from ever happening again?

- How do we replicate what we just did for the next time?

- Should we build or buy our way to expand our service offerings?

- How do we finance an expansion strategy?

- Given our budget, how do we accomplish our objectives?

- How do I progress my career?

List 3: Examples of Specific Day-to-Day Activities for Which Critical Thinking Can Be Helpful

- Assembling or fixing something
- Attending meetings
- Assessing risk
- Coaching
- Conducting brainstorming sessions

- Creating and interpreting surveys
- Creating presentations
- Engaging in financial planning activities
- Engaging in one-on-one conversations
- Evaluating proposals
- Making go or no-go decisions
- Organizing
- Planning your schedule/calendar
- Preparing speeches
- Prioritizing
- Reading (Are you paying attention to the underlying meaning of the words?)
- Reviewing contracts
- Reviewing spreadsheets
- Setting goals
- Setting metrics
- Teaching
- Writing (e-mails, directions, proposals, reports, etc.)
- Writing and conducting performance evaluations

The Takeaway

Critical thinking can be applied everywhere in your business and life, but be selective. Use critical thinking when the outcome might make a difference.

3 The Framework and Tools

In this chapter, I introduce a simple framework to guide you through the critical thinking process. The framework, which provides tools and techniques, consists of three components: clarity, conclusions, and decisions.

Clarity

The single most important reason why headscratchers—projects, initiatives, problem solving, decisions, or strategies—go awry is that the headscratcher itself—the situation, issue, or goal—isn't clear in the first place. Clarity allows us to define what the issue, problem, or goal really is. For example, instead of a broad general statement, such as "We need to improve our quality," a clearer statement might be "We need to reduce our defect rate to less than 10 units per 1,000."

Conclusions

After you are clear on what issue you must address, you have to figure out what to do about it. Conclusions are solutions and a list of actions (to-dos) related to your issue. For example, "To reduce our defect rate, we will add a product test cycle prior to shipping."

Decisions

Once you come to a conclusion about what actions to take, you have to actually decide to take the action—and do it. For example, "The vice president has approved implementing the product test cycle before shipping, so we will start tomorrow morning."

Most people combine conclusions and decisions when they're asked about problem solving or decision making, saying, "I need to decide what to do." However, it's important to separate conclusions and decisions, because the thinking processes for each are very different. For example, you probably have a to-do list of your tasks. You haven't decided to do them yet, because if you did, they would not be on your to-do list; they would be on your done list. Although you might be the one who is responsible for coming up with a solution or a conclusion, you might not be the decision maker; it might be your boss.

To review, the critical thinking framework is a three-step process, as illustrated in Figure 3.1.

- *Clarity:* Get clear on the issue, problem, or goal; our company calls it the headscratcher.

- *Conclusions:* Take your clear headscratcher through the process of coming to a solution about what to do.

- *Decisions:* Take each one of your conclusions and decide to do it or not do it; to act, or to not act; to go or not to go.

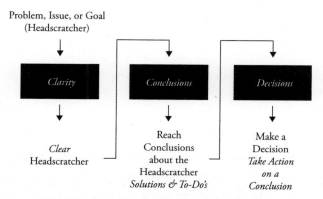

Figure 3.1 The Three-Step Critical Thinking Process

What's the difference between this process and the way we usually think? Usually, when faced with something new, you'll ask a few questions (*clarity*), then think awhile and come up with a solution (*conclusion*), and eventually make a decision and act (*decision*). But here is how critical thinking is different.

Our regular automatic thinking doesn't focus much on clarity and thinking. We spend a little time there but usually move to conclusions and decisions as quickly as possible, often spending plenty of time thrashing around. There are four reasons why we tend not to spend much time on clarity:

1. *We're not taught to think too much.* We're taught to *do*, and do quickly. Think about most of the tests you took throughout your education, starting from kindergarten through your upper grades. Tests took the form of you being presented with a problem that had four possible answers. Only one answer is correct, so your job was to pick the right answer quickly and go on to the next problem. But the world doesn't really work like that. When you face a problem, there are multitudes of ways to address it. You have to compare these choices, pick the most appropriate solution for your situation, and explain why. Although what we learn in school is helpful, we're not taught to think; we're taught to get to *do* quickly.

2. *You aren't paid to think.* As a former executive, I managed hundreds of people to whom I often said, "I pay you to think." However, the truth was that I paid people to get things done. Admittedly, thinking helps doing, but you are paid for actual, tangible results of that thinking. Imagine how your boss would respond if he asked you on a Friday afternoon, "What did you do this week?" and you answered, "Well—I thought a lot." Chances are that response wouldn't go over too well.

3. *You get personal satisfaction from* doing, *not thinking.* People don't get excited when they put something on their to-do list; they get excited when they get to cross it off. You get your personal satisfaction when you get things done, not when you think about them.

4. *You discover many things you don't know.* Although this might seem like a good thing, it does expose your ignorance, or your lack of knowledge. There's nothing wrong with this, of course; it's how we learn new things. However, many people are not okay showing others—especially their manager or peers—what they don't know.

These reasons mean that you spend as little time as possible in the clarity and thinking stages when you are in your automatic mode—and usually try to make a decision as quickly as you can. Usually, a few things happen when you do this, none of which is very desirable. You make a bad call, spend an inordinate amount of time trying to figure things out, and realize you're really not very clear on the matter at hand, or you solve the wrong problem—and then get to do it all over again. You waste a lot of time, money, and effort.

Critical thinking requires that you spend more time in the clarity phase, using a tool set. As a result, your conclusions come faster *and* are more accurate. Subsequently, you make decisions more quickly, because decisions in critical thinking are go or no-go calls; that is, all the work has already been done.

Consider the following: If you erected a building or baked a layered cake, which shape in Figure 3.2 would you prefer to use?

Although you invest more time in clarity during critical thinking, it usually takes less *total* time to make a decsion. Problem solving generally speeds up, and the quality of your solutions is enhanced as well.

Automatic Thinking

Critical Thinking

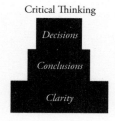

Weak foundation for decisions, less time getting clear, and more time needed for decisions

Strong foundation for decisions, more time on getting clear, and less time needed for decisions

Figure 3.2 Automatic versus Critical Thinking

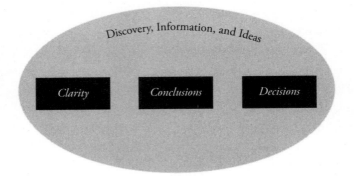

Figure 3.3 The Critical Thinking Framework

The space around clarity, conclusions, and decisions in Figure 3.3 is filled with *discovery*, *information*, and *ideas*. These three concepts include asking questions, exploring ideas, listening to responses, and conducting research.

The Takeaway

The framework for critical thinking is simple:

- *Clarity:* You *get clear* on the headscratcher.
- *Conclusions:* You create a solution for the headscratcher.
- *Decisions:* You take action on your conclusion.

    Within each of the framework components of clarity, conclusions, and decisions, there are numerous critical thinking tools and techniques to guide your thinking. As you use and practice these tools, your problem-solving and decision-making skills will improve. This will directly yield higher quality problem solving, decision making, and creative results.

Now to begin. We start with *clarity* and the tools to get clear.

Section II
Clarity

*C**larity*, the first and most important step in critical thinking, is about understanding the issue, problem, goal, or objective—the head-scratcher that you're looking to solve. If you're not clear, you risk solving the wrong problem. For example, let's say you have to fix a customer problem. What happens if you don't have a clear idea of the problem that customer actually has? You might spend a good deal of time and effort attempting to solve something that wasn't a problem in the first place. Although your customer might really appreciate your effort, you haven't solved the headscratcher.

Here's a specific example: It's Monday morning at 11:00 AM. You're in Los Angeles, waiting on a flight scheduled for an 11:30 AM departure to Dallas. You have a business meeting that starts at 7:30 AM on Tuesday. You hear an announcement: "Folks, we have a mechanical situation on the plane, so I'm afraid this flight is cancelled." You and 200 other people make a mad dash to the customer service center.

After you wait in line for what seems like forever, the customer agent, who is unbelievably polite and empathetic, gives you the good news: "We've automatically booked you on the first flight out tomorrow morning."

You respond, "That's just not going to work. I have a 7:30 AM meeting tomorrow. Is there any way you can get me to Dallas today?"

The agent responds, "There's a flight through Chicago that leaves in 50 minutes. You can connect to a flight to Dallas at 5:30 PM, arriving at 8:00 PM. Is that okay?"

You say, "Yes!"

Although the agent initially had a solution for getting you to Dallas, *that* wasn't your problem. Your problem was getting to Dallas *today* so that you could (1) get some sleep and (2) make your meeting tomorrow.

Without clarity on an issue, you risk redos, mistakes, and even addressing a *symptom* of a problem but not actually solving the headscratcher.

In this section, we'll introduce 10 tools you can use to get clear. In many instances, you'll probably use only a few at a time. Some you'll use more often than others, and as you practice, you'll probably favor a few. It doesn't matter how many or what tools you use; the objective is to get clear. We'll explain each tool, provide you with examples of using it in your work, and close each chapter with a few exercises to practice. In the last chapter of this section, we'll summarize clarity and the tools that I presented.

The Takeaway

Spend some time getting clear on the headscratcher you are solving—even if you think you already are. A small investment in clarity at the beginning of the process can save a tremendous amount of time and effort later on, because it minimizes the possibility of having to go back and start again because you were unclear.

4 Empty Your Bucket

The Bucket

The first tool I introduce for critical thinking and clarity helps you get your head in the right place. We all have a *bucket* that contains the memories of our experiences: past projects, interactions with other people, or attempts at solving a problem. When you encounter a situation that is similar to one you remember, many of the memories you first invoke tend to be negative. Specifically, they focus on why this prior task was unsuccessful or the constraints and barriers you faced. Figure 4.1 shows what a typical bucket looks like.

The problem is *there is no room in a filled bucket for critical thinking and creativity*. You can't think critically or be innovative from the perspective of the memories in your bucket— because it's filled with prior experiences that significantly affect the way you reach conclusions. If you're thinking from the perspective of the things in your bucket, then your conclusions are going to be heavily biased based on those items. As a result, your breadth of conclusions will be narrow. If, however, you understand and can learn to ignore what's in your bucket, then you're much more likely to be able to create *new* conclusions.

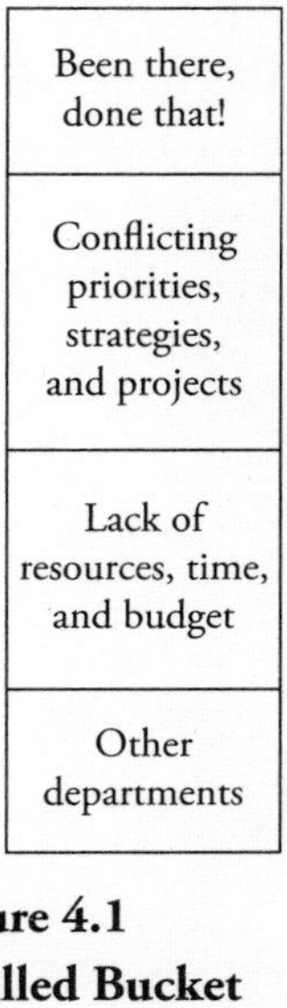

| Been there, done that! |
| Conflicting priorities, strategies, and projects |
| Lack of resources, time, and budget |
| Other departments |

Figure 4.1
A Filled Bucket

For example, let's say senior management issues a directive about a project that they've labeled as a top priority. Perhaps you have had experience with this statement, and your initial reaction is something like, "Yeah, this and every other project. I'll just wait a few days to see if the priority changes." We don't want to discount your experience; you might be perfectly correct. This is your knee-jerk reaction, and maybe it's accurate; in a few days, the project's urgency *will* pass. *However,* suppose this time the project truly *is* a priority. Then you've made an assumption based on past experience that's to your detriment. If you empty your bucket, forget about the past, and take a closer look at what this issue is, you'll get a better idea about what's different this time. One way to do this might be to ask a few questions about this project's importance relative to the other projects on which you are working.

When looking at a headscratcher, you must have the attitude of *there is always a way*. Although this might not *always* be the case, you're much more likely to find a way if you start by believing there's one. You're putting yourself at a disadvantage if you approach the headscratcher with the moaning-and-groaning-filled bucket containing the stories of how something didn't work in the past.

Of course, you can't wipe out your memories, nor would you want to. Many of your memories are good ones you don't want to throw out, and many contain useful information you'll want and need to call upon. What you want to do is *understand* what's in your bucket and how those memories might be affecting the way you think.

Figure 4.2
An Empty Bucket

How do you empty your bucket and prevent those experiences from adversely affecting your thinking? There's always a way. Think, for example, of someone in the past for whom you cared dearly, who may have had a significant health issue, economic hardship, or difficult family or social situation and managed to work through it, perhaps someone such as a cancer survivor. Think about the problems that individual had to endure and solve. Now realize that if he or she can solve that problem with all those hardships, surely you can solve your problem despite—and occasionally with the help of—the items in your bucket.

Admittedly, you might have some pretty huge items in your bucket. Perhaps a business partner once conducted shady deals behind your back, leaving you with trust issues. Maybe you've had a history of running out of time on certain projects, or your team has consistently run over budget. Not all bucket items are easy to overcome. But there's a much greater chance of doing so if you think in terms of "There's always a way," as opposed to "I can't do that."

Getting Started with *Emptying Your Bucket*

Here are a few situations where you can start emptying your bucket:

- *In meetings:* Listen to the conversations. When you hear the bucket items coming out, such as "We tried that before" or "Here we go again," it's time to give a little speech. Perhaps make a short comment: "Folks, I know we have seen this situation before, and perhaps this time we will end up with the same result. We have a choice. We can all sit here moaning and groaning, or we can use our heads and figure out a way to solve this problem. Although we might not be successful, we're more likely to figure this out by *trying* to figure it out, than by just talking about why we couldn't figure it out the last time."

- *Before a conversation:* Prepare to have a conversation, not with the memories of conversations gone bad, but with the optimism that this time it will be different and productive.

- *When curbing your initial reaction:* We tend to interpret e-mails, memos, and conversations immediately with respect to the memories in our bucket. This might result in a very positive or negative reaction, and neither might be warranted. Remember that your brain discards and distorts things, and you may have misinterpreted the situation. If your enthusiasm is premature, you'll probably recover from your disappointment. However, if you err with a negative reaction, you can do some serious morale and credibility damage. Approach the issue with an empty bucket.

The Takeaway

Innovative solutions require open minds, empty buckets, and a tenacious belief that a satisfactory solution exists. Never give up. Be persistent. Now you can start to think critically and get clear.

Exercises to Help Empty Your Bucket

1. Before you approach a problem to solve, or if you're currently engaged in this process, spend five minutes and write down all the items you think are in your bucket that might be influencing the way you think about this particular problem. Include both those that negatively and those that positively influence you.

2. Consider the items you listed in the first exercise, and write about why each might be in your bucket. What experience, or experiences, formed it?

3. Listen carefully to the conversation during your next meeting. Do you hear the items that are in other people's buckets? What can you do to help empty them?

4. Share and acknowledge your bucket by saying something like, "Here's what I've experienced that makes me feel this way about this issue and why." Once you understand your bucket, then you can start challenging it by asking, "How would my view of this situation change if that bucket item didn't exist?"

5. What story or event in your life are you going to use when you get bogged down in your bucket? The answer is the story that will have you say, "Gee, if I/they were able to solve that problem, then I will be able to solve this problem"; in other words, "There is always a way."

6. When someone says to you, "Yeah, we tried that a half dozen times already," how are you going to respond?

7. Prepare a three-minute speech on the notion that "There's always a way." Give a few examples of a goal thought to be unreachable that was somehow achieved. Cite specific times when everyone was down and defeated, and then someone came in and was able to use a new idea to solve the challenge.

8. Listen to others' frustrations and make a list of what you think is in their buckets and why. Then, ask them. If you're going to help others empty their buckets, you have to know what's in there.

5 Inspection

A great way to start getting clear after emptying your bucket is to engage in some inspection. This is simply the act of determining what all the words in a given headscratcher mean and ensuring all the parties involved in solving it are operating according to these same definitions. This simple technique can generate some amazing discussions when a group of people gets together to define words such as *better, faster,* or *quality.*

Here's a simple example: Have you ever had a passenger in your car while looking for a space in a parking lot? While you're scanning for a space, you're also watching out for people walking and other drivers dashing through the lot. Your passenger shouts out, "There's a spot over there!" Now you either have to take your eyes off where you are driving to look where your passenger is pointing or have to ask, "Where is 'there'?" It would have been much more efficient if your passenger had said, "There's a spot one row over to the right and four or five cars ahead of you." Although these words take more time to say than "over there," they are much clearer, and the result will be a faster understanding of the situation—and a parked car.

Here's a common business example: *we need to improve the quality of our services.* Just about every company we work with has this goal. Let's take a closer look at this statement:

- *We:* Who are *we*? Your group? Your department? Everyone in your company? Does that include your partners, vendors, and suppliers—or perhaps even your customers? Consider it from another perspective: Have you ever said, "We need to take out the garbage when we get home"? Are *we* the entire family, your spouse and yourself, one of your children, just you, or just your spouse? If you are not clear on who *we* are, everyone might think it means someone else. In this instance, confusion over *we* results in the garbage not being taken out at all.

- *Need:* Is this a need or a want? This is a huge distinction. People tend to use "I need" or "We need" interchangeably with "I want" or "We want" all the time. In critical thinking, we use the term *necessary*—because it's hard to mix up *wanted* with *necessary*. We'll cover *need* in its own chapter, but for now, the important thing is to determine whether something is necessary or wanted. Of course, you want to improve service to your customers. But that's not the question. The question is, is doing so necessary?

- *Improve:* Improve to what? How do you plan to measure whether quality improves? If you can't measure it, how would you *know* you improved it? Let's say you manufactured 1,000 widgets per day, and 75 were rejected because of defects. Your manufacturing manager might say, "We need to improve our yield," so someone might start an initiative to improve. Two weeks later, the average rejection rate after manufacturing 1,000 widgets is 74 per day (down from 75). That's technically an improvement, from 75 to 74 defects, yet that's likely not what management meant by *improvement*. If the manager had been specific—for example, if he or she had said, "We need to bring our defective rate down to 25 per 1,000 widgets"—not only would the goal be clear, but employees also could have launched an appropriate initiative to achieve that result.

- *Quality:* What's the definition of quality? It's however *you* define it. If you're working in groups, it's what the group agrees it to mean. Let's say you're working with three other groups, and each has a different definition of the word *quality*. The result is likely to be many misses. And when people have a different definition for *quality*, they probably have a different definition of the word *done*. "I'm done!" someone exclaims, and others look at him in surprise, saying, "No, we don't think so; you have to document your work."

- *Our services:* Does this mean every service; every touch; all the things your company produces, resells, distributes, and represents? Or only some of them? And what *are* the services? Answering the phone? Updating and maintaining your website? Staying on top of your delivery schedule? Getting 10 out of 10 on a survey?

Developing a clear understanding of the terms eliminates confusion and ambiguity. Even when you are working alone, you can think critically and inspect your problem statement. Don't just wave your hands and say, "Yeah, I know what I mean." If you claim that, you won't be nearly as clear on your issue as you would be if you sat down for a few minutes and wrote down what you actually mean.

Getting Started with *Inspection*

Here are a few simple places you can get started on *inspection* right away:

- *E-mail:* Everyone reading this book probably writes at least a few e-mails a day, perhaps dozens or more. The next time you write an e-mail, ask yourself before you hit Send, "Is what I am about to send clear? Could any of the recipients of this e-mail misinterpret what I mean?" Suppose your e-mail said, "We need to get this done faster!" Instead, you might say, "It takes us ten days to do this, and we need to do it in seven days." It's a little bit more precise and certainly clearer.

- *Meetings:* Meetings are a great place to utilize inspection, because people throw all kinds of words out in meetings. Someone might say, "We need to reduce our spending on this project." Ask for clarification on *reduce*—reduce the total spent to what, and over what period? Does *reduce* mean fewer people or less capital? Does *reduce* include reducing the scope of the project, too?

- *Goal setting:* Inspect the words you use when setting goals. How would you measure achievement of that goal? What do you mean when you say something like, "I would like to improve my performance"? There's a difference between *would like to* and *have to* (want versus need). Also, what do *improve* and *performance* mean to you? Both words are very vague. If you spend just a few minutes developing a clear meaning of these terms, you'll save a tremendous amount of time later. You'll also know you're addressing the right issue.

- *Provision of instructions:* Everyone knows that when instructions are not clear, the appropriate results are not achieved. An example is having to assemble a piece of furniture, a toy, or an appliance but the instructions are unclear.

- *Requirements for review:* Much like unclear instructions, unclear requirements lead to deliverables that most likely miss expectations. Unclear product requirement documents is one of the major causes of product delays.

- *One-on-one, crucial, and hard-to-have conversations,* such as a performance improvement plan: Clarity can prevent misunderstandings and continued problems.

The Takeaway

Eliminating the ambiguity and interpretation of words will go a long way toward achieving clarity and focus. Use inspection to understand the meaning behind words and ensure a common definition among a group.

Exercises for Inspection

1. Rewrite these sentences so that they are clear:
   - "We need to get there faster."
   - "Our project is behind schedule."
   - "If we had more resources, we could get this done on time."
   - "Try this again; only this time, do it with quality."
   - "The brochure you are creating should have a blue cover."
   - "I'll get back to you soon on that issue."

(*continued*)

(continued)

- "Don't worry; I have it under control."
- "Please call these customers and find out what they want."
- "You need to document your work."

2. Reread the last three e-mails you wrote. Rewrite them to be clearer.

3. Look at the last three e-mails you received. Do you understand all the words? Is it possible you might misunderstand something? If so, what question(s) might you ask to get a better idea of what the sender meant? Did you ask those questions?

4. Take a look at the goals your manager sets for you or that you set for others. Are they clear? Are they specific? Is there ambiguity in how they would be measured?

6 Why?

Why *Why?*

Why? is the most powerful question you can ask during the critical think- ing process. Asking why results in answers that provide us with knowledge, thereby giving us choices, and as Sir Francis Bacon said, "Knowledge is power." Knowledge lets us be more creative, solve problems, and make better decisions.

For example, let's say that someone asks you to move all the furniture in one room to another. You might ask, "Why?" and discover the carpets are getting cleaned tomorrow. Once you know this, you would make sure to move the furniture to a room without a carpet.

For a more complex example of *why*, imagine you're in a meeting to discuss making a particular process faster. You might typically create a pro- cess flow diagram and then discuss how you could eliminate or streamline some of the steps. This would certainly lead to a faster process, but imagine if you asked, "*Why* do we want to speed up this process?" That conversation might lead you to discover that the real objective is to ensure timely delivery of products to your customers. This knowledge might prompt you to suggest—in addition to speeding up delivery with this faster process—you can make a huge difference by looking at how you forecast product demand so that you know what to make in advance.

In this chapter, we'll cover four reasons why we ask why. But before we get into that, we need to look at what happens when you ask why. Let's say your manager asks you for a report or information on a project and you respond by asking, "Why?" He'd likely interpret your response negatively—as though you're questioning the request, being insubordinate, implying that you think it's a bad idea, or simply not caring. But that's *not* what this *why* is.

Your *why* really means, "To do the best job I can, to accomplish what you need, and to make sure I provide you with the information, product, or deliverable to address what issue you have, I need to understand more about what you are asking. So, why do you want that report?"

You ask why:

- to distinguish *this* from *that*;
- to find a root cause;
- to get to "I don't know"; and
- to get to the *double because* (Because!!).

Let's look at each of these list items in more detail.

Ask *Why* to Distinguish *This* from *That*

Have you ever been asked for something or to perform a task, and got a response similar to the following when you delivered it: "Oh, that's not what I needed," or "That's not what I asked for"? Perhaps you delivered what was requested, but the requestor asked for something else later on because he or she realized what was asked for initially wasn't what was needed in the first place. Not only is this a waste of time, but it's also frustrating.

Consider the following simple example: A man asks you for a roll of tape. You give him a roll of tape. He comes back and asks for more tape. You give him more tape. He comes back and asks you for some string. You give him string. Then you see him carry out a package that has all kinds of tape and string on it. Your reaction might be, "Oh, if I had known you needed to ship a box, I would have just given you the premade shipping boxes with the packing tape stored over here."

Here is a slightly more complex example: A manager asks, "Can you please run a report showing the sales of each product for the past four months?" You run the report. The manager subsequently asks, "Now can you show the sales of each product by salesperson?" You run that report. "Now, can you do one for the marketing programs that have been approved for the next six months?" You run that report, and as you deliver the report, you notice that your manager is creating a PowerPoint presentation titled *Sales Forecast*.

You say, "Excuse me, but are you requesting this data so that you can create a sales forecast?" Your manager confirms. You reply, "Oh, if that's what you want to create, you might want the product release schedule over the next six months, because we are updating many of our products and expect a significant increase in revenue."

Interactions such as these happen all the time. We often ask others to do something without bothering to give them the reason *why* we want those actions performed. Although it's not practical to explain yourself every time you ask for something, it is prudent to do so when it's for a substantial issue or problem. If you ask someone to make a copy of an invoice, you need not explain why—as long as it doesn't matter to you that it might end up being a black-and-white copy on regular paper. However, if you asked someone to make a copy of a presentation for you, explaining you want the copy for an executive leadership presentation might ensure your copies are in color, on bond paper, and bound.

As you can see from both of these examples, knowing the *why* at the beginning would have made a big difference in how a person approached these tasks—and likely would have made the overall process much more efficient for everyone involved.

When someone asks you to do something—run an errand, create a report, call a customer, start a new initiative, revise a product, check a reference, create a schedule, or just about anything else—our company calls the request asking for *this*. In other words, "Please do *this*," "*This* needs to happen," or "Can you do *this*?" You might be given a list of *this*'s. All of these are instances in which you should ask *why?* Specifically, "Why do you want this?" or "Why are you asking for this?" or "Why do this?"

Again, you're not questioning the person's *reason* for asking; you're just trying to get a better understanding of the issue. You're looking for the person to say, "I need you to do *this* because I need *this* in order to accomplish *that*," or "We need *this* so we can figure out *that*." In the previous example, when the manager asks for a report, that's the *this*. "I need this (report)." If asked why, the response may have been, "Because I'm creating a sales forecast." The sales forecast is the *that*. It's the real headscratcher. Running a report is just a to-do item. *That* is what you want to learn about—because *that* is most likely the real headscratcher this person is looking to solve. *This* is usually just a to-do, a task required to accomplish *that*.

Once you understand what *that* is, your response might be, "Oh, if *that* is your issue or problem, then not only do you need *this*, but you also need this other report," or "Oh, if you want to solve *that*, then *this* isn't what you need; you need this other thing over there." Last, you might respond, "*This* is exactly what you need to solve *that*."

Figure 6.1 is the image we use to describe the relationship between *this* and *that*. It illustrates multiple *this*'s (to-dos) that might be requested. You then ask *why* to discover *that*, the *real* headscratcher to be solved.

Figure 6.1 *This* and *That*

The Takeaway

Asking why helps distinguish *this* from *that*—and although *this* may be an important step, *that* is the headscratcher. Why allows you to uncover other issues and helps determine whether the problem for which you are seeking answers (*this*) is the real headscratcher to be solved (*that*).

Ask *Why* to Get to a Root Cause

We also ask why when we want to understand an event that has occurred: something breaks; a customer cancels his or her account; a vendor is late on a deliverable; or we miss a schedule, lose a sale, or exceed our budget. The event could be a positive, too: we beat the forecast, completed the project ahead of schedule, or increased our customer count. We group these events together as "This result happened."

We use why to drill down until we reach a root cause. You ask, "Why did this happen?" The response you are looking for is "Because of that." Then you ask, "Why did that happen?" You anticipate the response "Because of that other event." Additional probing with *why* will get you to a root cause—the initial decision, failure, or event that eventually led to the result. It could be a successful result you want to duplicate or a result you want to prevent in the future.

Here's an example: You print a document from your computer, but when you go to the printer, there's nothing there. You go back to your machine and try it again, making sure you're sending to the right printer. You go to the printer, and the document is not there. You ask why and discover the printer is out of paper. You put paper in. Lots of other things are printing, and you figure these are other people's jobs that have been stacking up—so you wait. The printer stops, and your document still isn't there. You ask why, because the printer seems to work, just not for you. You try printing to another printer, but nothing comes out. Again, you question why. You notice you have three documents waiting to print: the two you tried to print to the original printer and the one you tried to print to the other printer. *Why?* Finally you discover the problem: your computer isn't connected to the network. Asking why *again* helps you learn the network cable is not connected. You then remember that you took your laptop home last night to do some work and forgot to plug in the network cable when you returned this morning. You plug the cable in, and the printer starts printing your stuff. The failure to connect the network cable was the root cause of your printing difficulties.

Figure 6.2 illustrates how you drill down using *why* to find a root cause.

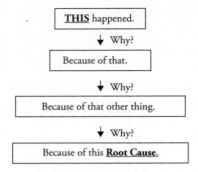

Figure 6.2 The Root Cause

Something happens: "This happened."

You ask, "Why?"

The response: "Because of that."

You ask, "Why?"

The response: "Because of that other thing."

You ask, "Why?"

The response: "Because of this."

You keep diving deeper until you find the root cause.

The Takeaway

Asking why—sometimes more than once—helps you discover a root cause. Knowing a root cause helps prevent undesirable results from occurring again or allows you to repeat a desirable result.

Ask *Why* to Get to "I Don't Know"

When you ask *why*, you may get the response "I don't know"—perhaps while asking questions as you look for the root cause:

"Why did that customer cancel?"

"I don't know."

"Why did that component break?"

"I don't know."

"Why don't we have enough candidates to interview?"

"I don't know."

Perhaps when distinguishing *this* from *that*, you ask, "Why are we doing this?" You might receive the response "I don't know."

Although it might seem like a lack of response, "I don't know" is actually a very important discovery. You want to continue to ask why to get to "I don't know," because you most likely need this unknown knowledge to achieve clarity on the issue. "I don't know" also clarifies the boundaries of knowledge you and others have about a situation. Get to "I don't know," but then find out those answers—because you *have* to know when it comes to critical thinking! A response of "I don't know" is a signal to ask other questions, such as:

"*Who* might know that you can ask to find out?"

"*How* can we find out?"

"Can we *make any assumptions* that will allow us to know and then validate or invalidate those assumptions later?"

You can't move forward when the situation is *I don't know*.

The Takeaway

Ask why to get to "I don't know," and then go learn what you don't know.

Ask *Why* to Get to *Because*!!

We call this the *double because*—a *because* with two exclamation points. It's a because you can't *reasonably* do anything about. For example, let's say you want to solve the following: "How can I make it easier to pay all my bills?" There are rent or a mortgage, taxes, and utility bills to pay; food, clothes, and gas to buy; and maybe even college or other school expenses. You surmise you could accomplish this if you didn't have to pay taxes. Well, having to pay taxes is a *because!!* You can march on Washington and try to get taxes eliminated, or you can break the law and not pay taxes. But assuming you don't do either of those, you have to pay taxes. You still have to solve your headscratcher. There's always a way; it's just not *that* way. Go bang your head against a different wall, because that taxes wall isn't moving. *Because!!* is a constraint to your solution.

If you work in a regulated industry, such as pharmaceuticals, financial, food, or communications, you have to abide by certain laws enforced by the Food and Drug Administration, the Federal Communications Commission, or the Securities and Exchange Commission, and numerous other local, state, and federal agencies. You might regularly hear (and ask), "Why do we have to do all this paperwork? Why do we have to fill in these forms, report all this data, or run all these trials?" It's okay to ask and even to push to discern whether these requirements are *truly* immovable. However, if the effort or timeline to alter these regulations is significant—or until the law gets changed—these are all examples of *because!!* You still have to get your project done, on budget, on time, and with the available people you have. There is a way, but it won't be by getting the *because!!* to go away.

> **The Takeaway**
>
> Asking why helps you get to *because!!*—which is a constraint to your eventual solution.

Getting Started with *Why*

You can use *why* in many circumstances to dive deeper into what the problem, issue, or goal is and get a clearer understanding of your headscratcher. Here are just a few examples of when you can use *why:*

- *When setting goals:* Ask, "Why is that the goal?"
- *When setting and evaluating priorities:* You want to consider why something is a top priority. Ask, "Why is that so crucial? Why is that more important than these other initiatives?"

- *When someone raises an issue as a problem:* Ask, "Why is that a problem?" This will allow you to discern whether it's really a problem that needs to be solved—or solved in the timeframe you've determined.

- *When something unexpected or unplanned occurs:* In this situation you might want to look for the root cause by asking, "Why did that occur?" or "Why did we miss that?"

- *When receiving or sending meeting invitations:* It's perfectly acceptable to ask, "Why am I invited?" Likewise, when you send an invitation out, clarify why you're having a meeting, why these people are invited, and what you expect them to contribute in the meeting.

- *When you see something you don't understand:* As in, "Why did they do that?"

- *When someone asks you for something:* Ask, "Why are you asking for that?"

- *When someone says, "We can't do that":* Ask, "Why can't we do that?"

Summary of Takeaways

Asking *why* helps you get clarity on your headscratcher by allowing you to:

- distinguish *this* from *that*;
- find a root cause;
- get to the *I don't know* and the things you have to find out; and
- determine whether it's a *because!!*

It might take 50 words the first time you use why, because you may have to explain *why* you are even asking. However, once others understand you are in critical thinking mode (headscratching) and appreciate the value of asking why, you can use a single, but powerful "Why?" It is the knowledge gained from the answers to why that helps you create solutions to the actual problem, issue, goal, or objective—the headscratcher.

Exercises for Why

1. Take out your to-do list and look closely at each item. Ask *why* you have it on your list. Once you answer the question, ask, "Are the items on my to-do list the only things I have to complete to fulfill my *why* for doing them?"

2. Do you have a list of requirements or specifications for a deliverable you are committed to? Do you know *why* those requirements are on that list?

3. Look at your goals. Why are these the goals you've chosen?

4. The next task you ask someone—a peer, subordinate, or family member—to do, explain why you are asking. Give him or her the opportunity to question why you want it done.

5. The next time you find yourself explaining to someone *how* to do something, think about *why* you do it that way. You may find no reason, other than you've done it that way before.

6. Look at the meetings to which you have been invited on your calendar. Do you know why you are invited, what is expected of you, and why the meeting is being called? If you called the meetings, do all the participants know why they were invited?

7 So What?

In the last chapter, we covered the critical thinking tool *why*. Another very powerful critical thinking tool, and my favorite, goes hand in hand with *why: So what?* Its place in critical thinking differs from its conventional use; here, *So what?* is *not* a question you ask if you don't care. Rather, you ask because you care a great deal. What you really want to know is, "What is the relevance of *this?*" or "What if *this* were to happen?" You're truly asking, "Why is this important?" Although that's a question with a *why* in it, you're really asking for the *so what*. However, you must take care when using *so what;* people could easily misinterpret it as your being a wise guy or insubordinate.

I can remember the very first time I asked, "So what?" A customer care manager came to me and said, "Mike, our call hold time (the amount of time a customer has to wait on the line until a customer service representative takes the call) is down to 15 seconds." I asked him if I should be happy or sad, and the manager responded that I should be happy.

I asked, "Why?"

The manager explained, "Because we answer calls in 15 seconds."

"So what?"

At that point, the customer care manager looked at me in confusion. The conversation continued. What was the value of answering the call in 15 seconds, when our nearest competitor took over 60 seconds? Will our customers buy more from us? Will they recommend us? Will we retain them longer? It was costing us a lot of money to answer calls that quickly; could we obtain the same result if we answered the call in 30 seconds? The answer was yes.

Because of what I uncovered in that instance, I began using *so what* every day. When someone came to me with a problem, I randomly asked, "So what?" I worded it in a very safe way; people knew it wasn't a challenge. It was merely a question to get people to think. That's just what happened: people started to think about the answer to "So what?" just in case I asked the question. When they thought about their response to it, they often figured out what to do—not every time, but very often.

For example, a team was running behind schedule on a project. The team leader said, "We have to tell Mike." Then they discussed what would happen if I asked "So what?" and they came up with a number of possible actions, deliberating everything from moving some resources around to cutting functionality to working overtime. Instead of coming to me and saying, "Mike, our project is running behind schedule," they said, "Mike, because our project is running behind schedule, we are going to move some people around. This will put us back on schedule for this important project. By doing this, we'll delay the start of that other new, lower priority project for a week. The ramifications of our delay (the *so what*) on the other project are virtually inconsequential. That project doesn't have a deliverable date yet, and it was already deemed an 'as time available' initiative."

I thought to myself, "Wow, these folks really thought about the *so what*," and replied, "Okay!"

If you're a manager, and you want to affect the positive performance of your group instantly, ask, "So what?" once a day. You will be absolutely amazed, but beware: you really need a *genuine interest* in helping people to think. Make sure your team knows why you are asking this question; they need to understand that it's not to trap them but to help them. Similarly, if you want to improve your personal performance, ask yourself, "So what?" before you go to someone with a problem, and think about what your response would be if your manager asked you, "So what?"

You ask, "So what?" to stimulate thinking when you or others have recognized a problem. This question generates conversations about importance, interdependencies, value, relevance, business and customer impacts, and cost and schedule impacts—just to name a few.

So What: Your Company or Product

Your company's *so what* is often called its value proposition. What is your company's *so what?* What value do you offer your customers? Is it price, service, availability, uniqueness, or all of them? Even if you sell bottled water, you have a value proposition. Perhaps it's the purity, the biodegradable bottle, a unique cap, the price, the distribution, or the availability. Successful products have a very quantifiable *so what.* No matter how cool or useful a product might seem, you should always identify the *so what* with respect to the value to the customer when developing it. If the *so what* is unclear, the product isn't likely to succeed.

Your *So What*

This is huge; some have called it life changing. What is *your so what?* What value do you provide to your peers, family, and company? What makes you, *you?* What skills, talents, and insights do you possess to allow you to accomplish the things you do? Identifying this *so what* allows you to hone in on the circumstances, problems, and issues to which you can add value. It helps you understand how you can apply your skills in different ways.

If you're happy in your job, one of the main reasons is likely that you are able to exercise your *so what.* I once gave a series of classes to professionals who were laid off titled "How to Use Innovation and Critical Thinking to Find a Job." Most of the folks in the class had had healthy and long careers but had found themselves jobless because of the economic meltdown in 2008/2009. People in the class had labeled themselves: "I'm a hydraulics engineer," "I'm a paralegal," "I'm an instructional designer," or "I'm a clothing fashion consultant." We spent a good deal of time attempting to discover each participant's *so what.* Take the hydraulics engineer. This guy was most excited when he explained his last job and how he kept the projects, no matter small or large, on task and on schedule. He was able to foresee issues and cut them off before they affected the schedule. Yes, he was a hydraulics engineer, but that wasn't his *so what.* He was a super project manager. He had a solid sense of organization, order, and how events impacted others. He was also very personable and could get others to be motivated to adjust what they were doing—that affected the schedule. He just happened to be applying his *so what*, his superior project management skills, in the hydraulics engineering field, but the truth was that he could apply that *so what* in nearly any field. Therefore, instead of limiting his search to a hydraulic engineering–related job, he broadened his search to super-project-manager-related jobs. This quickly expanded his universe of job opportunities.

What is your *so what?* What makes you, *you?* What do you love to do and do well? Whatever it is, it's been with you for a long time. What trait did you have as a kid that you still have—that you're still good at? That's your *so what*. Think about it this way: when you have a great day at work, you were able to apply your *so what*. Understanding your value like this can go a long way when looking at problems related to your career, your success, and your happiness.

Getting Started with *So What*

Here are a few simple places you can use *so what*.

- *Meetings:* Have you ever been in a meeting where one individual says something that doesn't seem to be related to anything being discussed? Everyone pauses to acknowledge something was said, but then the discussion continues where it left off. The impression of what was said is it was an irrelevant thought; you, and everyone else, throw that thought out. Remember: Our automatic brain often throws out things it doesn't think is important.

  Chances are that when someone says something in a meeting—however irrelevant it seems—he or she often sees a connection between what he or she is thinking and what is being discussed. The person isn't speaking up just to cause confusion. Instead of ignoring the statement, express your confusion, and ask for clarity. Say, "Excuse me; I'm not quite getting what you are saying. Can you say this in a different way so I can understand what you're thinking and perhaps get an idea of how it's related to the conversation?" If it was a random thought, there won't be a connection. But if it wasn't—and more than likely it wasn't—you've now brought new thinking into the conversation. Instead of everyone throwing out what was said, you've enabled that other person's thought to add value—by asking that person "So what?" (even though you never used those words). Ask, "So what?" in meetings. Although it might take 40 words to ask, it's important to get to the *so what.*

- *When the unexpected or unplanned happens:* Many opportunities to ask "So what?" fall into this scenario. Not only do you need to ask why something happened, but you also need the ramifications (*so what*). Ask, "So what?" about your customer calls, your competitor's new promotion, your project that's running behind schedule, or the increase in rent. You also want to ask it about the good things that happen: if you just got promoted or you face a new opportunity. Asking "So what?" motivates people to really think about what is important, what the consequences are, and how things relate to each other.

  Here's a simple example of the unexpected: one of the key members of your team calls in sick, and it appears she will be out of the office for the better part of a week. Your deliverable is due in two weeks. Asking "So what?" guides you to a conversation about how the missing team member will affect the deliverable, how you might compensate for that, or how your teammate might still contribute despite being sick. *So what* leads to discussions about who is depending on this person's work, how this might affect your group, and how it might affect those expecting the deliverable.

  When the unexpected occurs, *so what* generates thought. Because of that thinking, you generate ideas about dealing with the unexpected.

- *After receiving the answer to why:* After you ask why and get a response such as "Because . . .," try asking, "So what?" Again, you're not trying to be a wise guy; you're really asking: "What are the consequences, given *that* explanation for why? What does that mean to the project, the schedule, our people, our customers, and the costs? What's the relevance? What are we doing about it?"

- *When looking at reports, spreadsheets, and data:* Are you looking at information and asking, "So what?" What do the data tell you? What's important about the information in the spreadsheet or report? You may have seen project status reports where some items are in green (everything okay), some are in yellow (some issues), and some are in red (problem). Ask, "So what?"; in essence, what are people doing about the red items? How about the yellow items? Is everyone going to wait until the items turn red to do anything about them? Even consider the green items; what's the *so what* there? Why are things in good shape, and can you replicate the reasons why? Is there anything you should be doing to ensure the green items stay green? Additionally, I've seen status reports pages long and so confusing that I wasn't sure if it was a for your information, a to-do list, a cover your butt, or what. It is really beneficial to see the *so what* about the status. Are there actions I need to perform, watch, or worry about?

- *Lessons learned:* Many companies have formal reviews of completed projects, sometimes called lessons learned, best practices, or postmortems. One of the questions to ask about the findings is "So what?" What's the *so what* about a project that was behind schedule because something wasn't clear? Are you going to change your processes to prevent delays from occurring again or just hope they don't? If the project went really well, figure out why and what the *so what*—the takeaway, the learned experience—is that will allow you to repeat that success again?

- *New initiatives and prioritization:* A variation of the use of *so what* is to ask, "What's the value?" or "What's the impact?" How do we benefit from this new initiative? Knowing this helps you understand how the new initiative relates to the business. If you're a manager announcing a new project, instead of just giving people another thing to do, it's valuable to communicate how this new project will affect the business (the *so what*) or other projects and initiatives.

- *New products and marketing strategies:* What's the product's value proposition—its *so what*? What customer problem does it solve? Is there some unique *so what* you can identify? Understanding a product's or service's *so what*, its value proposition, is crucial in marketing to customers and differentiating you from the competition.

The Takeaway

So what helps you achieve clarity on the relationship between the headscratcher you are solving, and others that may exist, and actions and their consequences. *So what* gets to the relevance, the importance, the value, and the impact.

Exercises for So What

1. Pick up any item on your desk—a piece of paper, a pen, a cup holder—what is the *so what* about that item? Why is it important? How is it relevant? What if it weren't there?

2. Break out your to-do list again. In the exercises for *why*, you asked why those items were on your list—which hopefully helped you discover what problem you were solving. Go back to that list now and ask, "So what?" So what if you fix that or do that? So what if you don't? You put it on your to-do list, but what happens if you don't accomplish it or get it done in the time you established?

3. While working or interacting with your colleagues, kids, or spouse, notice an accomplishment or something that surprises you—something positive. Ask yourself, "So what?" Should you highlight the accomplishment? Does the person you are interacting with understand the *so what* (the value) behind his or her action?

4. What is your *so what*? What makes you valuable to your peers, your family, or your company? What are the skills, accomplishments, or things that you have or do that make a difference?

5. Take a look at the specific steps of a process or procedure you have. What is the *so what* behind each step? Why is it there, what is important, what is the outcome, what is the consequence of complying—or not complying—with the process? Are people following it? If not, so what? What are the ramifications of noncompliance? Do they matter? Why?

8 Need

What Is the Necessity?

More than 2,000 years ago, Plato claimed that "Necessity is the mother of invention." If you want to get something done—if you *need* to get it done—then you have to understand why it is necessary. Think about how often we use the words *want* and *need* and how interchangeable we make them. We want lots of things. I want a new car, but do I need one? When getting clear about a headscratcher, ask why it is *necessary* to solve.

Think of a goal or task to do that you've had for a while. Do you ever think about why you haven't accomplished it—or even spent much time on it? I sometimes excuse that lack of progress on not having time to do it, but I have time. We all do. We just choose to spend that time on something else. I haven't accomplished it because the *need* to accomplish it isn't there. If it were necessary, I'd get it done.

Here's a simple business example: Many information technology (IT) departments send out periodic notices to employees to clean out their corporate e-mail inboxes, because e-mail takes up loads of storage. What do you do when you receive that request? You might delete a few e-mails, but you probably don't spend much time going through the old ones. Why should you? Where's the need? It's a request, a *want*—and although the IT department really *needs* to recover storage, or they will have to buy more, what's *your* need to help them with this? You don't have one in this regard until one day, when you get an "Inbox full" message. Guess what happens then? You're deleting old e-mails like crazy—because now, it's become necessary.

One of the most common headscratchers we encounter when training executives or managers is "How do I get my people to make more decisions on their own?" We usually engage in a brief discussion about how their reports always come to them for advice on every little thing. Inevitably, my response is, "Your people are not making decisions themselves *because they don't have to.* They come to you, and you give them the answers. You take the responsibility for what happens next, because it's your idea—so why should they? Instead, be available to help, especially on the bigger decisions, but make it necessary for *them* to make the call."

Have you ever asked a group of people a question and then been met with silence? What do you do? After only a few seconds, you rephrase the question, ask another question, give them an idea of the direction of the answer, or just answer the question yourself. Instead, what you should do is make it necessary for someone to think and then answer. The easiest possible way to do this is simply to shut up. You ask the question; then it's their turn. Do not speak! You are guaranteed to get a response. People *need* to put an end to the awkward silence that's now present. It works every time.

When we critically think about a headscratcher, we ask what the need is. Let's say your headscratcher is "We need to improve our response time to customers." As a critical thinker, you'll inspect the words, determine the why and so what, and then get to the need. Of course, improving response time would be great, but why is improving response time necessary? Will you lose customers if you don't? Will you fail to meet your objectives on customer satisfaction? If your answer is yes, then this objective is indeed necessary. But think hard about whether it's truly necessary. Our workdays are filled with a million things to do and figure out. I don't know anyone who says at the end of the day, "Gee, I don't have anything to do. I'm finished with everything." There's always *something* to do, and we generally have a limited amount of time to do it. This is what makes it so important to distinguish necessary things, those with the potential to make a real difference, from *wants* that won't contribute very much.

Ever see the same goals come back, year after year?

"We need to be more agile."

"We need to be more customer-centric."

"We need to grow revenue faster."

"We need to cut expenses."

Of course, you know from reading just a few chapters of this book that these goals are not clear at all. One of the reasons most people and organizations never achieve them is because everyone has a different interpretation of what each one truly means—thereby making their completion evasive. Another reason is that the *need* isn't clear, so when something with a clear need comes along, it takes priority—and trumps the time you'd use to reach these goals.

Priorities are sometimes set using the "who shouts the loudest" method, but the critical thinking method might start with understanding the need with respect to time. Is it needed? By when? Conversations about what will happen if the task or initiative isn't completed by that time will help flesh out needs versus wants.

Great Teams and Need

If you want to align people and get them excited, motivated, and charged to accomplish a goal, the greatest motivation you can give them is making it clear why it is necessary for them to accomplish the task.

Think about the best, most enjoyable, and most successful team on which you have ever been. What made it so great? One attribute we see in every case of great teams is that members have a common need. This ensures that everyone is focused, aligned, and marching to the same tune. Politics and personal agenda go away, and everyone is on the same page. Priorities are clear. Perhaps you have heard the expression "A team is gelled." Even opposing parties in a government seem to be more functional when the necessity is clear. It's when the necessity is unclear and in debate that things get ugly. If you're a leader who wants your team to be extremely productive and work together, make sure members are all executing a common need: not yours, but yours *and* theirs. You must all see and agree on the common need. Those companies possessing that clarity thrive.

One example of how powerful a common need can be took place in September of 1995, when the dial-up Internet business was exploding. (For the readers who grew up with broadband, the prior method of connecting to the Internet was via a phone landline—incredibly slow compared with today's connection speeds.) The norm at the time was to charge by the hour of usage. But then the chief executive officer of one of the largest Internet companies woke up one morning and decided to differentiate the offering, so he announced, "New pricing: $19.95 for unlimited usage." This took the vice presidents of the company completely by surprise. They thought it was a joke! But, no joke: the press release was already out. Even more unsettling, the announcement proclaimed the new pricing and packaging would be available by the first of January, a mere three months away.

After the senior team got over the shock and bewilderment at making this goal so public, they realized that this had to happen. It was *necessary*—and that need drove a remarkable sense of cooperation throughout the company. The silos of departments went away. *Your* responsibility became *our* responsibility. The teams helped one another, made compromises, moved people around—even got pizza for one another. The workload was intense, but the necessity of achieving the goal overpowered every obstacle, and the team was ready to launch the new service by the first week of January. Their focus to meet the need created a strong camaraderie and admiration among the team members, and many of the relationships established during those three months continue to flourish today.

Need and Survival

Of course, there is no better need to get people motivated than the need to *survive*. In 2000, I was working at a company that had fallen prey to the communications industry collapse. Prior to 2000, the availability of investment money to grow communications networks was like water pouring from a faucet. There were 50 medium-sized communications companies, all of which were spending investment money like there was no tomorrow. Then Wall Street investors did some math—and oops! The spigot was turned off completely. We needed a plan to become profitable, and fast. Of course, we had a plan before, but investments had been easy to get. Being profitable was a want—not a need. Now, if we didn't get profitable—and quickly—the company would liquidate. The need was simple: be profitable, or cease to exist—lose jobs, fire everybody, liquidate the assets, and say good-bye to customers. This need made many of our initiatives become clear—both those that we discovered no longer mattered and needed to be stopped and those that made a difference and needed focus, resources, and execution. Many of our competitors didn't recognize this need, and they certainly didn't get their employee base to recognize it. We emerged from bankruptcy; most did not. We succeeded because the entire employee base understood the common need: survival.

Here's another, much more extreme example of necessity: Do you think you can swim 10 miles in open ocean water? Most readers would say no and never even attempt such a crazy stunt. But picture this: You're out on a boat 10 miles from shore, and it sinks. Are you just going to raise your hands and declare it's time to die? I don't think so. You'll try to swim, and although you may not make it, you'll certainly die trying. Why? It's necessary. I bet you would swim a much longer distance than you have ever swum before—and maybe even make it to shore.

Getting Started with *Need*

Here are a few places you can use *need:*

- *Priority setting:* Understanding the need behind an initiative can help in setting priorities, especially in groups. Conversations about why something is necessary and what might occur if the initiative *isn't* a priority can take the emotional attachment out of this process.

- *Interdepartmental cooperation:* When departments are not communicating or cooperating well, look for the lack of a need or for multiple *needs.* If needs are aligned, then cooperation and communication happen, because both become necessary.

- *Timing and sense of urgency:* When you or your coworkers have a different sense of timing or urgency to get something done, then have a needs conversation.

- *Use of the critical thinking tools why and so what:* Inject a few "So why is that necessary?" questions into the conversation.

- *Leading:* Communicate the necessity of your goals. Why do you have to do it faster, better, and with higher quality? Give your employees the real reasons. If you're like Apple, maybe it's the need to be the best or to be different. If you're a pharmaceutical company, maybe it's the need to help people live better lives. If you're working on the manufacturing line of an airline or auto company, maybe the need is to prevent accidents and injury to your customers. Find and explain the common need; you'll see productivity, morale, and performance improve.

The Takeaway

Understanding and getting everyone aligned behind an initiative's *need* is crucial in ensuring that you're addressing the right problem, decision, or goal. Spend time at the early stages of problem solving by taking a close look at what the need is. Why is this necessary—for the business, as well as for each individual member of the team? Once you've vetted the need, you'll have a better understanding of the headscratcher—and the team will be aligned and successful.

Exercises for Need

1. Once again, go back to your to-do list. What do you have on there that isn't necessary? If it's not necessary, then why is it there? If you don't want to take it off, then there's probably a need. What is it?

2. Think about one thing you probably should have on your to-do list that isn't there: maybe something related to your family or a personal goal. Why is it missing? Understand if it's necessary. If not, then move on. If so, what about this issue makes it necessary to be on your list?

(*continued*)

(continued)

3. When you first get to work, make a list of things you plan to do that day. Indicate what the need is next to each one. What happens if it doesn't get done today?

4. Take a look at your team and those teams with whom you interact. What is the need of your own and other teams? Are they consistent? Synergistic? Contradicting?

5. The next time someone has a conversation with you, ask yourself what the person's need is. Is there a problem he or she wants you to solve? Does the person need your opinion? Does the person just need you to listen? Is he or she simply looking for companionship? What is the need behind the conversation?

9 Anticipatory Thinking

What's Next?

Imagine the following scenario: you're at home with a significant other who says, "Can you please go to the grocery store and get a dozen eggs?" You agree and drive to the grocery store for some eggs. Shortly after you return, your housemate says, "We have that party to go to tonight. Can you please pick up the dry cleaning?" Again you agree, and off you go to retrieve the dry cleaning. As you return to your house, you start thinking about that party and realize you probably should bring a small gift. Out you go again, back to the grocery store, to buy a thank you card. Later that evening, you and your housemate get in the car to drive to the party. You notice the gas gauge is low, and although stopping for gas will make you a little late, you have no choice but to stop at the gas station.

Rewind. Imagine if the conversation were this: "Can you please pick up a dozen eggs, and while you are out, can you also pick up the dry cleaning, because we have that party tonight?" You then think to yourself, "Hmm, party tonight. I probably should pick up a card while at the grocery store and check to see if I need gas. I can fill up at the same time." Imagine how much time you would have saved!

Anticipatory thinking is a way to stimulate thinking about consequences and related tasks that you may not have initially contemplated. Basically, it entails asking what's next. What's after that? What will happen if I do this? What might be the reaction if I say this?

How many times have you said to someone, "If you do that, then someone's going to get hurt," "If you do that, then the customers will not be happy," or "If you say that, I'm taking cover, 'cause you're going to get your head handed to you"? Instead of those warnings, ask, "What will happen if you do that?" This will prompt the person who is about to take that action to do a little critical thinking on his or her own to determine the likely consequences of his or her impending action.

Architects are a group of professionals who are constantly asking what's next. A database architect will not just look at immediate requirements but will also ask, "What do you think you'll want three years from now?" A building architect might question, "Are you planning on putting a swimming pool on the roof?" They ask questions such as these because if they designed a building that someone wanted to add to later—for example, put a swimming pool on the roof—there's a good chance they'd have to change the design to provide more support for the structure. If the building is already in progress, that's a very expensive alteration.

Here I always recall the Boy Scouts' motto, "Be prepared," because anticipatory thinking is all about *being prepared*. If you're going camping, you may anticipate weather changes and bring appropriate clothing. How about when giving a performance review? If you're a manager, one of your responsibilities is to give feedback to your employees on their performance. Many managers will write reviews but never ask themselves the question about what's next. If the performance review highlights some areas of improvement, the next step is to provide suggestions as to how the employee can accomplish that growth. If an employee is demonstrating superior performance, it's a good idea to point out how he or she can influence other members of the team.

One of the more impactful applications of asking what's next is in the arena of business development, particularly product development. I've seen countless companies reap the benefits of a very successful product offering only to squander their lead because they didn't anticipate what was next. Customers' needs change, and so do their requirements for new solutions.

The companies who continue to innovate are always asking, "What's next?" and "What's after that?" High-tech companies, such as Google, Apple, and Amazon are always asking what's next. Retailers, such as the Gap, are asking what's next when it comes to clothing trends. Auto companies are looking at what's next both in transportation needs as well as in alternative fuels and electric cars. Home builders ask what's next not only with respect to materials, room layouts, and kitchens but also about built-in Wi-Fi or even fiber optics: "If we come out with this new offering and it's a hit, then our competition will be sure to jump on it. What do we plan to do when that happens?" and "How are our customers evolving—what's next *for them?*"

One more situation where you want to ask "What's next?" is in looking beyond your company and seeing what's coming to the world of technology, operations, medical procedures, manufacturing methods, leadership techniques, motivation and incentive trends, health care solutions, and more. You want to be asking constantly: What are people out there working on? What solutions, although not available today, will be available tomorrow, next month, or over the next few years? It's incredibly valuable to get a notion of what's coming next in the supply chain, the components that you use in your products, or the applications and tools that your company might use to solve a future problem.

For example, in 2011, Boeing began commercial flights of its 787 Dreamliner aircraft. One of the highly competitive aspects of the Dreamliner is its fuel efficiency, partly because of the use of the lightweight, yet stronger than aluminum, carbon fiber materials. Years before the Dreamliner's launch, Boeing's engineers were certainly looking out for new materials that they could use to reduce the aircraft's weight while improving its strength. You can be sure that someone was asking, "What's next in materials?" when pondering that question. As a result, Boeing took the lead in the use of carbon fibers in aircraft with its exciting Dreamliner.

Most people are naturally good at anticipatory thinking and answering what's next. The problem is that we don't ask that question often enough—at least, not in a professional setting. But think about all the anticipatory thinking you do when driving your car. You're looking ahead at people in a crosswalk; at the possibility the traffic light might change to yellow or red;

and at the cars to your left and right, in back and in front of you, and at the intersection, anticipating the possibility that someone might do something stupid. When you do this, you're thinking—even in your automatic mode—about all the things that might happen next. You're good at this. You just need to learn to apply the same thing to critical thinking in your business world. You can do it by asking the question "What's next?"

Getting Started with *Anticipatory Thinking*

Here are a few places you can use *what's next:*

- *When someone communicates a new task or initiative to you:* When you get or delegate a responsibility, are you asking (or communicating) what might be next? People will execute their initial task differently if they know what's coming down the road. Knowing what's next after your current task will change how you work on whatever that particular thing is. For example, if you know after you complete a project you'll need to document the steps you have taken, then you will keep track of those things as you accomplish your task. This is much easier than having to search your memories for all the details long forgotten.

- *When people who have a lot of responsibilities or roles add yet another to their plate:* Say, for example, that your college kid proclaims that he's going to join another intramural activity. You might just want to ask what's next by saying, "Sounds interesting. How will that affect your study or your 15 other activities?" Also, you can use anticipatory thinking when you get additional professional responsibilities. How is this going to affect your other work? Let's say that you are promoted to a manager position, asked to lead a new team, or moved to a new company in a leadership position. You might use anticipatory thinking to consider your direct reports' perspective and get some idea about what they might be wondering. Anticipate that they are asking themselves about what you are like, what you are going to change, and how it's going to affect their job and current projects. You'll be prepared to answer these questions if you ask yourself, "What's next after I start this new job or position?"

- *When you are interacting with customers:* Good salespeople always agree with their prospective customer about what the next step is. What's next makes it clear to all parties who is to do what, and, importantly, *when.* It moves the ball forward. You can apply this with your customers, on projects, and in teams by asking everyone involved what his or her next step will be.

- *In meetings:* Before you end the meeting, ask what's next. Is there an action list? A follow-up? Who is accountable for what?

- *When prioritizing:* Map things out: do this first, then this, then that, and so on. Ordering with respect to "This has to come after that" can help as an efficiency tool.

The Takeaway

To provoke anticipatory thinking, ask *what's next*—or "What consequence might this action cause?"

Exercises for Anticipatory Thinking

1. Go back to your to-do list. For each item, ask yourself, "After I complete that, what's next?"

2. In the next meeting you attend, take note of whether there is a "What's next?" discussion at the end. If not, consider starting one.

3. Think when you write your next e-mail about whether there's a "What's next?" message after that. If so, is there a way to combine the two to be more efficient?

4. When you arrive at work, create your to-do list—but also put it in order of your priorities. You'll be using anticipatory thinking during that process.

10 What Else?

What Else Could This Be?

We've already determined that one reason to ask *why* is to get to a root cause. *Why* did something happen—or what could explain why something happened? *What else* is another tool used in this discovery. When ideas start to subside, asking *what else* stimulates lateral thinking with respect to new possible explanations. *What else* is a tool to prevent coming to a premature conclusion about what happened—or what to do next.

Physicians use *what else* often when diagnosing a medical issue. When you visit a doctor and are displaying obvious symptoms, it would be easy for him or her just to say, "Oh, you have a cold." Asking "*What else* can cause these symptoms?" could lead to a blood test, strep test, or other questions, such as "Do you have any pain *here*?" *What else* continues the investigation—and allows you to discover *other* potential causes.

A very effective way to ask the *what else* question is to say "What else could *possibly* cause this?" The word *possibly* opens the door to ideas, no matter how remote, that could be a cause. In your automatic mode you might typically discard such unlikely causes, but in critical thinking you consciously evaluate them.

What else can also acknowledge a good idea while keeping the conversation going. For example, why was your product launch so successful? One response might be: "Because we had it so well organized and orchestrated." Your response might be: "Okay, is there *anything else* that may have contributed to success?" Someone might add: "Because we applied the lessons from the last launch and this time staffed the phones at a level no one thought we would need, but ended up using." Keep probing: "Okay, anything else?"

When people communicate, they often surprise one another with their reactions. It's called a *miss on anticipatory thinking:* "Gee, I *thought* they would be happy to hear this." You might ask yourself, "What other (*what else*) interpretation might be going on here? What else are they involved in that could have changed how they viewed this?"

Getting Started with *What Else*

Here are a few places you can use *what else:*

- *When you want to augment inspection with* what else: When defining words, ask *what else* they could mean. How else could this be interpreted? What other meanings could be attached to these words? For example, someone might define *quality* as a measure of defects. Asking what else *quality* means might result in conversations about ease of use or availability of customer support, or how to buy or maintain a product.

- *When you think you know the reason for something:* Keep thinking about what else could have caused this thing, or is causing it, until you've exhausted possibilities.

- *When you thought you knew the reason for something:* When you investigate the cause that you think is responsible for something and discover that it isn't the cause, it's time to ask, "What else could possibly cause this?" There is *always* a cause for things that happen, so if your initial evaluation fails to result in identifying the cause, keep asking *what else*.

- *During brainstorming:* Use *what else* to encourage new ideas, new concepts, and new explanations. Ask questions such as "What else do our customers ask for?" or "What else can we do on our vacation?"

- *When building or designing something:* Ask, "*What other (else)* ways can we accomplish this?"

- *Augment what's next with* what else: When asking *what's next* or what the consequences for a given action might be, ask *what else* to stimulate thinking about additional *what's next* items or consequences.

The Takeaway

Ask *what else* to keep the thinking going, to stimulate new ideas and new possibilities, and to prevent premature closure of an issue, idea, or solution.

Exercises for What Else

1. Think about a goal you have and the things to do related to that goal. Ask *what else* you should be doing.

2. The next time someone says, "I think I know what's going on," listen to his or her explanation and ask, "Could there be anything else that caused this?"

3. Look at the last five e-mails you wrote. Other than what you intended, *what else* could they be interpreted to mean?

4. Pick up any item your desk. What is it used for? Write down 25 other possible uses for that item. Keep asking yourself, "What else?"

11 The Ingredient Diagram

Ingredients of Your Headscratcher

If you were asked to bake a chocolate cake but weren't sure what the ingredients for this particular recipe were, how good a cake could you bake? It probably wouldn't be that great. Similarly, if you're going to solve a problem, but you're not clear on the variables affecting the problem, how good a solution do you think you can create?

The *ingredient diagram* is a tool that helps you transition between clarity and conclusions. At this point, you're still getting clear on the headscratcher. However, you are also now starting to get ideas about where to look for solutions. The ingredient diagram helps you understand the variables defining your headscratcher. Your solution will incorporate all, or many, of the variables.

Here's a very simple example: Your car has a full tank of gas. You're planning a long road trip during which you will need to stop for gas. There are many variables that affect how far you can go with a full tank of gas. You look at a map and ask yourself, "Where along the route should I stop?" One of the key ingredients of this headscratcher is your car's miles per gallon (MPG) rate. Without determining this ingredient (variable), your solution won't have much of a basis. Another variable is your speed. The rate at which you're driving will affect how often you'll need fuel for your car. Other ingredients might be how much traffic there is, how many passengers you are carrying, whether you are hauling a trailer, and your tires' air pressure. To a lesser extent, you might consider the wind speed and whether you're driving into or against the wind. If you knew all of these ingredients, you could calculate a very accurate solution for when you should stop for gas.

A headscratcher's ingredients are the variables that define it. It often helps to draw what's called a fishbone diagram (called this because the sideways tree branches look a little like a fish skeleton). For the preceding headscratcher, the distance you can travel before having to stop for gas, the diagram might look like Figure 11.1.

The distance you can travel before having to stop for gas is a function of the following high-level ingredients: the car's rated MPG, the weight of the carload, and the car's speed. If you traverse the branches for each of these, starting with MPG, you're looking at the ingredients that make up MPG. In addition to what your car manufacturer rated the vehicle, your individual MPG will also be a function of the traffic you encounter and whether your car is in tune or needs maintenance. Moving along the ingredient diagram, look at the ingredients for *traffic*. This might include the day of the week and the time of the day. Similarly, you would fill in the branches for *weight* and *speed*.

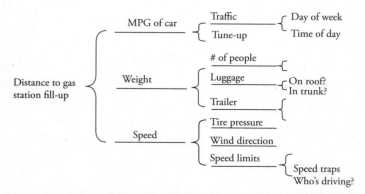

Figure 11.1 Distance to Gas Fill-Up—Ingredient Diagram

A few comments about the ingredient diagram: first, it can continue for pages. The preceding example was very simple, but if your headscratcher is how to improve productivity and you created an ingredient diagram for *productivity*, it has the potential to go on for many levels and pages. You know you're done with a branch when the terms on it repeat or are used on another branch or when there are no longer any additional ingredients to specify on that branch. For example, along the *weight* branch, because an average weight is a numeric value, there are no additional ingredients beyond that.

The solution for when to stop for gas has the ingredients shown in Figure 11.1. If you want just *any* solution, you might use the rated MPG of your car—and there's your answer. If you want a *better* solution, then you continue. The more variables of the ingredient diagram you take into account, the more accurate solution you will have.

Try this for yourself. Here's a headscratcher: How do I get my kid to clean up his room? This falls into a broader category of headscratchers about how you get someone to do something—with the operative word being *get*. You ask yourself: What are the variables to get someone to do something? If you want your kid to clean his room, you might have to give him an *incentive* (ingredient 1)—perhaps money or a privilege, such as permission to play outside. You might have to say something, such as "If you don't clean up your room, you can't watch TV." This would be a *consequence* (ingredient 2). You might have to give the *reason* (ingredient 3): perhaps you're having relatives visit. Go ahead and draw an ingredient diagram for *get*. In the end, you might have to implement *all* the ingredients to get the results you're seeking.

Now for something more complicated: improving your productivity. Let's begin an ingredient diagram for productivity (Figure 11.2).

As you can see in Figure 11.2, the ingredients for productivity generally include the following elements: the *amount of work* you have, the *time* it takes to do it, and the *quality* of the work you produce. Moving along the branch of *time*, the ingredients here are your *manager*, because he or she can give other tasks (*distractions*), take things away, and change priorities. (You can fill in the diagram with more specific details.) Your time is also

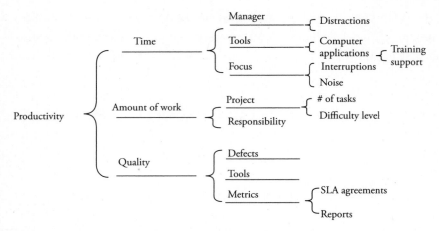

Figure 11.2 Productivity Ingredient Diagram

a function of the *tools* you use. Whether your computer is slow or fast or whether you have the right applications and know how to use them will all affect how much time something takes. Later in the tree, you see *training* under *applications*, because you need to be trained to use the applications; additionally, *support* is there because you need to get questions answered quickly. Your *focus* is also an ingredient of *time*. When you can focus with no *interruptions* and low *noise* levels, you get far more done. For an exercise, keep going with the productivity ingredient diagram.

Of course, if you want to improve your productivity, getting a faster computer might help somewhat. However, a much more comprehensive solution for improving productivity will include all—or at least many—of the variables that define productivity in the first place.

The next step in the ingredient diagram is to assign weights to each ingredient. In the sample when to stop for gas ingredient diagram, the car's MPG rating will be much more important than the wind direction or the number of passengers you're carrying. Assigning weights allows you to prioritize where to spend your time as you start to create solutions. Make sure your solutions incorporate the heavily weighted ingredients. In the productivity example, you should weight the applications you use more heavily than getting a slightly faster computer. The ingredients with greater weight will have a greater influence on solutions.

Getting Started with the *Ingredient Diagram*

Here are a few places you can use an *ingredient diagram*:

- *When you don't know where to start:* If you think you're clear about a situation but have no idea where to start to think about it, begin with an ingredient diagram to define your headscratcher's variables. Your starting point will become clearer.

- *During brainstorming and in group participation:* The ingredient diagram is a great place to discover new definitions and interpretations for getting clear on an issue with a group. In the case of "We need to improve our productivity," you might have two diagrams—one for *productivity* and another for *improve*. Then you can begin to ask specific questions: What do we mean by *improve?* What would the variables (goals, metrics, monitoring, corrective action, etc.) be?

- *When figuring out who to get involved:* In getting clear on and subsequently solving a problem, it's necessary to involve the right people. Perhaps one of the ingredients in a headscratcher about improving productivity is incentives. An ingredient of incentives could be rewards, as well as the human resources (HR) department (because it would need to approve them). Therefore, creating an ingredient diagram on productivity helps you discover that HR needs to be involved. Getting HR's support early to help identify possible solutions would be far better than informing the department after the fact about something it can't approve. Your ingredient diagram may uncover the need to get various people or groups—colleagues, vendors, or even your customers—involved sooner in the process.

- *When figuring out where to put your energy:* When you fill in your ingredient diagram, you'll assign weights to the ingredients. Ingredient 1 might weigh very heavily in your headscratcher, whereas ingredient 2 might not. This will help you determine where to put your focus and energy as you look for solutions.

> ### The Takeaway
>
> The solution to a headscratcher will incorporate the variables (ingredients) that define the headscratcher. Use the ingredient diagram to uncover what those variables are.

Exercises for the Ingredient Diagram

1. Create an ingredient diagram for learning to ride a bike. What are the ingredients involved in this process? (Hint: Bike, training wheels, parent, practice, support, and Band-Aids.)

2. This is a tough one: create an ingredient diagram for *communicate*, in the context of how to communicate better with peers in another department. What are the ingredients here? (Hint: What do you want to communicate? What are some ways to communicate [e-mail, phone]? Is this communication one-way or two-way [listening]? What do relationships have to do with it?)

3. Group exercise: With a few of your peers, create an ingredient diagram for "What should we do for lunch?" (Hint: Cost, number of people, time, distance, appetite, and cuisine.)

4. Create an ingredient diagram for *automate*, in the context of what you can automate in your business that you do manually now.

12 Vision

What Is Your Vision?

The last tool I'll introduce for clarity might actually end up being the first you use. It's a description of your *vision* about your headscratcher solution. You simply answer the question "What does the world look like after you solve this problem?" Describe the end state; then ask whether, given your vision, is this headscratcher the only thing you have to solve? If the answer is no, then what other headscratchers might you need to solve to make the world look like the one you envisioned?

Having a vision conversation can be both enlightening and depressing. On the plus side, you articulate what you're trying to accomplish—the big picture, the main goal. However, you generally end up with a list of headscratchers to solve after having this conversation. Sometimes, you'll have started the process with one problem only to realize you have a whole bunch of problems—a list of issues you need to solve to reach your vision. It's deflating, but with that always-a-way attitude, you will pick one to start with. You should reexamine your list at this point and make sure the headscratcher you've chosen to tackle first will have the most impact on your vision. If not, switch to another.

For example, let's say your headscratcher is "How do we improve our productivity?" You use the common tools—*inspection*, *why*, and *so what*—and at one point, you ask what the world will look like when productivity improves. You surmise that you'll create more functional and higher quality products in half your competitors' time—thereby doubling your market share. That's a lofty vision. Is improving productivity the only headscratcher you need to solve to reach that goal? No. Others might be:

- How do you shorten your product development cycle by 50 percent?
- How do you ensure your products fulfill customers' needs?
- What tools and methods will keep your defect rate less than one part per million?

Given the vision and new list of headscratchers to work on, you are in the position to ask one more question: If your vision is as described, are you starting with the right headscratcher—or might you make a greater impact by starting with another?

Articulating your vision and relating it to headscratchers is a great tool for aligning teams. The vision defines a common need and definition. As a result, you develop a true understanding of whether people are doing the appropriate work—that which contributes to the achievement of the *vision*.

Getting Started with *Vision*

Here are a few places you can use *vision:*

- *To get clear on the purpose:* When someone asks why about an initiative, one potential response is to relate that initiative back to the vision. If the person understands the vision and the relationship to the initiative is clear, then you have answered the *why.*

- *To set the stage for goals and problem solving:* As a leader, you may have a vision of what you want to happen or what you want your team, department, division, or company to achieve. However, you may not have a list of specific problems to solve to achieve it. Once you communicate the vision, you can then engage others to help figure out what headscratchers you need to solve to accomplish that vision.

- *As a gatekeeper for initiatives and problems to solve:* When someone comes forward with a new idea, goal, or set of initiatives and subsequent problems to solve, you can use a vision conversation to determine whether you need to allocate any resources. The question to ask is "How does this new objective contribute to achieving the vision?"

- *As an artificial need:* Needs don't have to be real, but they must be *perceived* to be real. As you read in Chapter 8, it's crucial to identify *need* to ensure things get done. One way to generate a need is to paint a vision so exciting and desirable that it becomes an emotional need. This can provide a very strong connection for people involved. For example, "We want to achieve a reputation as the most valuable and highest quality call center in the world." If your employees really want that emotional accomplishment, then it becomes an emotional need—which is as good as a material one.

The Takeaway

Using your vision to describe the end state helps bring out other initiatives, problems, issues, and decisions to consider. Sometimes you'll change your focus to work on something with more impact.

Exercises for Vision

1. Write down your vision for your retirement. What headscratchers need to be solved to accomplish that vision?

2. Does your team, your department, your division, or your company have a vision? If so, list your top three priorities, and explain how they contribute to that vision.

3. What is your 10-year vision for your career? What headscratchers do you need to solve to accomplish that? Are you working on any of those now? If not, why not?

4. What are some *needs* associated with some of the preceding visions, for example, your retirement? One need might be to take care of yourself and your spouse with food, shelter, and health. Another might be to be able to visit your children, and another could be a need to be intellectually involved in something. Try using the ingredient diagram tool to map out other needs.

13 The Thinking Coach

The Role of a Thinking Coach

Before we close the section on clarity, I want to introduce the very important concept of a *thinking coach*. This person plays a valuable role throughout the entire critical thinking process but is most necessary during clarity. Although you don't have to be a thinking coach to be a successful critical thinker, it's important to master this position if you want to help *others* think critically.

Your responsibility as a thinking coach is to get others to think and answer questions so that they can achieve clarity and generate ideas. You do this by asking questions—but there's one important caveat: *you cannot comment on their answers*. You don't make suggestions. You don't smile, wince, or judge responses. During clarity, your job as a thinking coach is focused on only one goal—for the person you're coaching to get clear. For example, if *faster* is defined as "one more than I'm doing now" for the person you're coaching, and that's clear, then all is good—even if *you* think it should be five more. In this scenario, your opinion doesn't matter. You must take the indifferent attitude of "I really don't care what your problem is or how you solve it; I only care that *you are clear about your problem*."

Being a thinking coach is actually much easier if you *don't* have any experience with the problem, because you won't be tempted to make suggestions or advise. When you have been through or have deep knowledge of a certain situation, it can be difficult to sit back and listen to someone think about it aloud. After all, we like to help. You get the urge to say, "Hey, how about just doing it this way?" But imparting your own view won't do anything to help the other person think and gain clarity.

Why Be a Thinking Coach?

If you're in a position of leadership, management, or supervising; if you run meetings or projects; if you have children or peers who look to you for advice—then one of your jobs is thinking coach. If you can do this, then you've taught a tremendous skill and have performed a great service for your student. Your reward? When others are thinking critically, they'll get more work done, with better quality—*and* you won't have to think as hard, because others are thinking, too.

Examples of a Thinking Coach

Let's say someone says to you, "I have a goal to increase my productivity." As a thinking coach, you might have the following exchange:

"Why do you want to accomplish that?" (*Why.*)

He answers, "If I can do more, I'll get more responsibility."

"Why do you want that?"

"It will mean more money."

"So is that your goal?" You might also ask, "How would you define *productivity*?" (*Inspection.*)

"Getting more work done in a shorter period."

"Is there anything else?" (*What else?*) Ask this person to map out all the things *productivity* means to him (*ingredients*).

In essence, you are using critical thinking tools without mentioning critical thinking. You ask questions, and he or she gets clear. Of course, it's far easier if he or she knows about critical thinking. Then you can just say, "Hey, let's use some critical thinking; I'll play the role of a thinking coach"—and off you go.

If You Have the Experience, Why Not Communicate That?

Your goal as a thinking coach is to pull ideas from the person you are helping. You will likely come to a point when you wonder: Is it easier, more efficient, and sometimes better just to give an answer? After all, if you've done something a hundred times, why go through the agony—and risk—of the other person's learning curve?

Your experience is one of the most valuable assets you have—so there's nothing wrong with communicating your experience and giving advice. Just know that when you do that, you have changed roles. You are no longer a thinking coach; you are part of the headscratching team. That's a good role, too, but it's not a thinking coach. There are only two reasons to be a thinking coach:

- To teach how to understand and analyze a problem using critical thinking

- To generate an idea about which you have not thought or an idea about something you don't know

If your goal is to solve a problem quickly, your best play is to be part of the problem-solving team, not a thinking coach.

Ten Rules of a Thinking Coach

Here are 10 rules for being a thinking coach. You must obey all of them to fulfill this role appropriately:

1. Explain your role as a thinking coach.
2. Don't take on this position if you are in a rush.
3. Only ask open-ended questions.
4. Pretend you know nothing about the subject matter.
5. Don't ask questions that lead the other person in the direction of your idea.
6. Always wait for an answer to your question.

7. Listen to the response and ask clarifying questions.

8. Allow the person you are helping to think out loud.

9. Keep in mind that *all* responses have merit.

10. Know that if you comment or give an idea or a suggestion, your coaching session is over.

Getting Started with *Being a Thinking Coach*

Here are a few roles fit for a thinking coach:

- *Facilitator:* Help one or more people get clear on an issue in a head-scratching (critical thinking) session.

- *Self-coach:* When you want to think critically, and there's no one to help you, you have to become your own thinking coach. You can ask the tough question, but then you have to answer. (Note: This application requires an extraordinary amount of self-discipline.)

- *Homework helper:* If you have kids who ask you to help them with their homework, is it better to give the answer or help them figure out how to get to the answer? This is a situation where you need to be a thinking coach.

- *Manager, supervisor, and leader:* When someone comes to you for help, advice, a solution, or an opinion, you have the option to give just that; or, you can talk about how to figure it out. If you want the latter, have a thinking coach session.

The Takeaway

The role of a thinking coach is to get others to think. Leave your ideas behind, and only ask questions. Use the tools of critical thinking. Wait for answers, and ask more questions.

Exercises for a Thinking Coach

1. Let's say an employee comes to you and says, "Hi, boss, can you tell me if this is the right approach to solve this problem?" How would you answer this question?

2. How about this one: "Hi, boss, I have a problem communicating with Department X. What should I do?" (Hint: Don't ask, "What do you think you should do?" because that's the same question the employee asked. Start with one of the critical thinking tools, maybe by asking, "What do you mean by *communicating*?" or asking a *so what* question, such as "Why is that a problem?" This is phrased as a *why* question, but you're really asking *so what*—so what is the ramification of not communicating well with Department X?)

3. You want someone to think about the risk associated with something. Besides asking about risks, what questions might you ask?

14 Summary of Clarity

Clarity: Getting Clear about Your Headscratcher

This section introduced a set of tools to help you get clear on your headscratcher. When thinking critically, you must plan on spending more time on clarity than you are typically comfortable spending. In fact, you and others may become restless—and someone might even say, "Can we move on now, solve the problem, and stop talking about it?" Remember, we don't like to spend too much time on clarity because we don't like to think that much; also—it's hard. Getting clear is not easy. It not only takes discipline, but it also can be deflating, uncomfortable, and frustrating. You get bunches of "I don't know" and sometimes "I don't care!"—but it's crucial to be clear. The single biggest reason why projects, initiatives, and goals fail is the headscratcher wasn't really clear in the first place. Get clear, and stay the course—it'll benefit you in the end.

Getting Started

Start with small stuff when you begin to implement critical thinking. Don't try to solve world hunger right out of the gate. Start with getting clear on your own personal communication, perhaps by deciding that you want to start writing simple, short e-mails. Use *inspection* to determine how to do this. Expand to meeting invitations; use *why* to articulate the meeting's purpose. When attending meetings, use *inspection*, *why*, and *so what*. Of course, be cautious about how you ask those questions; don't ask for clarity on every sentence in a meeting. Ask once, maybe twice—then stop. Others will catch on. Then use critical thinking on more complicated situations, such as project requirements and priorities. You'll love the results that come with thinking critically. You'll find that if you start a little at a time on the small stuff, you'll see the impact—and you'll definitely want to do more. Then you'll expand its use.

Practice

Just like any skill, critical thinking takes practice. You can't read a book about something and simply be good at it. We ask people to practice every day— but only for 5 or 10 minutes—on the small stuff first. After all, when you learned to ride a bike, you practiced on your street and around the neighborhood; you didn't practice by entering the Tour de France! When I say *practice*, I don't mean stopping your work to do so. Rather, it's practice that involves your work. You can do it as you are writing e-mails, as you prepare for conversations, and while you are in meetings. Ask small, short questions.

You'll practice only one tool at a time. Some of the tools need more time, such as the ingredients diagram, but that too can be rehearsed practically. Don't feel you have to fill in pages and pages of the diagram. Start at the high level first, and then stop.

It's also essential to practice *with someone*. If you're the only one you know who read this book, just paraphrase some of the tools for someone, and work with that person to practice. Grab a colleague and work together to define what *faster* means in the context of your work. Once you've practiced, you are ready to apply critical thinking to the big problems.

Clarity: Not about Solving the Problem

There's an overwhelming desire to solve the problem in the clarity stage. Many ideas about how to do so will come to mind, especially when you get into tools such as *why* and the ingredients diagram. These ideas might be great ones, or they might not work at all. Write them down and keep a list, but *don't* close off the clarity process. *Keep getting clear.* Too often, we implement an early conclusion, only to fail because we were still unclear as to what the problem really was.

When Am I Done with Clarity?

This is a great question—and one with no definitive answer. There is no formula for problem solving. If there were, we'd plug the world's problems into the formula, and we would have no problems. There are only ways to look at problems that generate ideas for solving them. Similarly, there is no definitive stopping point for getting clear. It's a judgment call. However, there is one rule that can aid your judgment. You are ready to move on when you can answer yes to this question: "Do the participants discussing this headscratcher all have a consistent definition of what it means, why we are working on it, who should be involved, why it needs to be solved, and what success looks like when it's solved?" In other words, have you spent time asking a sufficient number of questions about what the headscratcher really is? If the answer to that is yes, then you are clear (or certainly clearer than if you answered no). Then it's time to move on to conclusions and determine how to solve the problem. There's a test you can use to gauge clarity: ask all the participants discussing the headscratcher to write down what they each think the problem is (not the solution but the problem). If everyone writes the same thing down, you are clear!

However, the critical thinking process doesn't guarantee you've left clarity for good once you move on to conclusions—nor can it guarantee that your solutions are correct. It does, though, greatly increase the probability you won't have to revisit the issue and will come up with quality solutions the first time around. When no one is still scratching his or her head about the headscratcher, then everyone is clear, and it's time to move on to conclusions.

Can I Use Critical Thinking by Myself and Not with a Group?

The short answer is yes; however, it takes an extraordinary amount of self-discipline to be successful. You have to be brutally honest with yourself.

When you ask yourself why something is important to solve, you just can't brush off answering questions with "Because it is." Answer the question as if you were talking to someone else. That's the value you miss when you're doing this alone: there's nobody to keep you honest, to ask you the hard questions you don't want to answer. If you're capable of splitting your personality to play multiple roles, you can be successful. The person asking the questions is Person A. The person who answers them is Person B. Just don't let either role intimidate the other!

The Takeaway

The single most important reason why projects, initiatives, problem solving, decisions, tactics, and strategies go awry is that the head-scratcher wasn't clear in the first place. Getting clear is the first step in the critical thinking process and will help you and others understand a goal or problem.

Section III
Conclusions

You learned in the last section that clarity is of primary importance. If you're not clear, then you're apt to solve the wrong problem. You also learned a variety of tools that help you think critically and get clear. Although it's great to be clear, being clear doesn't pay the bills. The end goal is to *solve the problems* about which you've gained clarity.

Now it's time to come up with ideas, solutions, and to-dos relative to your headscratcher. Solving problems, looking at situations creatively, and making an ultimate decision about them is all about *coming to a conclusion* about an action to take regarding your headscratcher.

As such, this section will describe in detail how a particular set of eye-opening tools helps you, me, and everyone else come to conclusions—solutions and to-dos—for our headscratchers. As you will read, everyone arrives at conclusions the same way, but our personalities influence that process. Our beliefs and values play a role in everything we do.

Of course, we don't solve problems in a vacuum; we do so with other people—even if your only objective is to persuade them to embrace your opinion. When you understand conclusions, you can persuade and influence others more easily, simply by using that comprehension. In this section, you'll learn critical thinking skills you can use for persuasion. We'll also cover subjects such as outside-the-box thinking and how to generate creative ideas beyond your own experiences.

We hear all the time how it's bad to assume and how we shouldn't jump to conclusions. Forget about those expressions. They are very misleading and are the complete opposite of what actually benefits us. However, there is a huge distinction between automatic thinking and critical thinking in terms of making assumptions.

If you get one takeaway from this entire section, remember this: *it's all about the premise!*

In the following chapters, I'll detail the five components of the premise that forms the basis for most conclusions. These five components are facts, observations, experiences, beliefs, and assumptions. Unlike many stand-alone clarity tools, these five conclusion tools group together. Let's define them first and then put them together with examples and exercises.

15 It's All about the Premise

Deduction

Greek philosopher Aristotle is often credited with being one of the first to document reasoning that mirrors what we call deductive reasoning today. Plato and Socrates are also in the mix of deductive reasoning creators, and there's early Egyptian and Babylonian evidence providing support for even earlier uses. The truth is, whether it was documented or not, humans have used deductive reasoning for many millennia.

Here are two simple examples, perhaps from the time of cavemen:

"When water falls from the sky, and the pond fills with water, I have water to drink. Water is now falling from the sky, and the pond is filling with water, so I will have water to drink."

"When I touch a fire, it hurts. There is a fire over there. If I touch it, it will hurt."

Some modern examples:

"When my global positioning system (GPS) says to drive a certain route and I drive a different route, my GPS says, 'Recalculating.' Oops, I just missed my turn, and I'm going to drive a different route; therefore, my GPS will say, 'Recalculating.'"

"Every new employee must go to new employee orientation. We just hired a new employee, so he must go to new employee orientation."

"I'm holding a cup of only red marbles. If this statement is true, any marble I take out of the cup will be red."

The initial statement in deduction defines a general truth. Based on that truth, we can determine a specific instance is true as well. The classic example: all people (persons) are mortal (the general truth). I am a person; therefore, I am mortal (the specific).

With deductive reasoning:

- Everything is black and white. There is no gray; there is no uncertainty. It is either true or false; there is no sometimes, maybe, or depends. There is no discussion needed.

- No one will ever say, ". . . but . . ." There are no buts. If the initial statement (the premise) is true, then the conclusion will always be true. There is no argument, no debate, and no doubt.

Unfortunately, most events in our lives are not black and white. Our days are filled with maybe, depends, and sometimes. Even the expressions we use containing *always* and *never* are usually not absolute; we typically mean "almost always" and "almost never."

Also, because there are not many absolute truths out there, we don't get to use deduction very often. You've likely heard the expression "The only things certain in life are death and taxes." Well, we know some people don't pay taxes—so that leaves death as the only certain thing. All people die at some age; I am a person; therefore I will die someday. Maybe that's true today, but you can argue even that truth isn't absolute, as medical and technological advances progress.

Induction

Inductive reasoning also has a long history. In early years, it may have been applied like this:

"When I place the remains of an animal carcass outside my cave, it usually attracts another animal that's good to eat. So, I'm going to place an animal carcass outside my cave, and it will probably attract another animal good to eat."

Here are more modern examples:

"The last 10 times I had a conversation with my manager, I got more work to do. I should have a conversation with my manager about this project, but that means I will probably get more work to do—so I'm not going in there!"

"In the past, our customer call center got many more calls when we raised our prices. We are raising our prices next week, so our customer call center will probably get more calls."

"When it rains outside during the morning rush hour, it takes me longer to get to work. The weather report tonight says it's going to rain tomorrow morning during the rush hour, so it will probably take me longer to get to work."

With inductive reasoning, the initial statement consists of a set of specific instances—many times, a set of experiences—that allows you to then generalize all future instances. The larger the set of repeating specific instances, the more confidence you'll have in it happening again.

Here's an example: A customer calls and says, "I think there is something wrong with your product. I took it out of the box and it was cracked." Do you go running to manufacturing, screaming that all of your products are defective? Of course not. However, what if you received 100 customer calls an hour, and everyone said, "I took the product out of the box and it was cracked"? *Now* you're probably headed to manufacturing faster than you can hang up the phone and say, "Thanks, let me look into that right away." One instance of a cracked product might just be a shipping accident; 100 calls per hour about cracked products means there's a good chance that there's a problem.

We call the set of initial statements or instances the *premise* (a customer called about a cracked product); the outcome (product is defective) is the *conclusion*. The stronger the premise (100 customers called with the problem, not just one), the more confidence in the conclusion (we really have a problem here).

There are a few important points to remember:

- When it comes to inductive reasoning, *the outcome isn't guaranteed.* There is only a *probability* that it will occur. In the preceding examples, another animal might not show up; your manager might not give you more work to do; or your call center might not get more calls this time. You're never absolutely sure.

- *Almost all* of your thinking is inductive reasoning. We come to thousands and thousands of conclusions a day using inductive reasoning. For example, your day begins by concluding to get out of bed.

- The *stronger* the initial statement (the premise), the *more probable* the outcome (the conclusion), and the *higher* your confidence.

Although few things are certain in our real world, many are highly probable. Unless something is absolutely certain, we use inductive reasoning to come to a conclusion. You make thousands of conclusions a day when operating in automatic mode—from what to wear and eat to which way to drive to what to say. You make nearly every one of these decisions via the process of induction.

It's All about the Premise

Remember, the stronger the set of initial statements (the premise), the more probable the outcome (the conclusion)—and the higher our confidence. The premise comprises facts, observations, experiences, beliefs, and assumptions (see Figure 15.1). It's all about the premise; this is where the process begins, and is the foundation of every conclusion you make. Although we still need to define the preceding terms, Figure 15.1 shows how you use each of these components in your premise and how a conclusion follows.

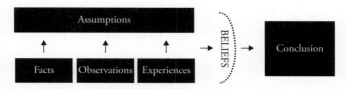

Figure 15.1 The Conclusion Process

You make assumptions using facts, observations, and experiences as the foundation. You then come to a conclusion that your beliefs have filtered.

We'll come back to this diagram in "The Conclusion: Putting It All Together" after we define these components.

The Takeaway

Almost all our thinking is inductive reasoning. The process starts with a premise composed of facts, observations, experiences, beliefs, and assumptions. The stronger the premise, the more confidence you'll have in the conclusion you form.

Now let's take a closer look at the five components of a premise—what we've been referring to as the initial statement—and how it all works. Ready? Let's start with facts.

16 Facts

Facts Are Absolute Truth

We define *facts* as "absolute truth" in critical thinking. With facts, there is no debate. You are reading this right now; that's a fact. Facts are *facts;* they aren't hearsay, opinions, or rumors.

However, when someone says, "Here are the facts," that doesn't mean what follows is factual. Remember the most recent presidential (or really, any political) debate? Both candidates stood up and said, "Here are the facts," yet they contradicted each other. Facts can't be contradictory if they are indeed the one and only truth. So the facts the candidates were throwing at us were not really *facts*. You could even read in the paper the next day how *un*factual their facts were.

When you hear something over and over and over again, you might mistakenly think it's a fact. When someone with great credibility says something, you might assume it's a fact. In either instance, it *might* be a fact—but unless you know the information to be true, it may not be.

Facts are a very important part of your premise. Because they are absolute truth, you can bank on, leverage, and state facts with confidence. It makes a premise strong. You can come to highly reliable conclusions if you base those conclusions on facts alone. Facts are often the basis for deductive reasoning. Although you don't get to use deductive reasoning often, when you do, it results in correct conclusions.

Mathematics is based on facts. Laws and rules are often used as facts. Science creates rules that, until proved otherwise, are considered fact.

Unfortunately, there aren't many facts. We can't be absolutely sure about the future, and because facts are absolute truth, *nothing* about the future is a fact. If someone makes a statement about the future, whatever it is, it certainly can't be a fact. For example, let's say the sun will shine somewhere on Earth tomorrow. Is that a fact? Although it is extremely probable, there is no guarantee the sun will be around tomorrow. It could explode, or an asteroid could destroy Earth tonight. Both scenarios are highly unlikely, but because they are both possible, they prohibit the statement about the sun shining on Earth tomorrow from being a fact.

Let's look at a statement. "I have a meeting tomorrow at 8:00 AM." Is that a fact? You might think so—but no, it isn't! There are a multitude of reasons why that meeting might not happen. If you said, "I have a meeting in my calendar that is *scheduled* to start at 8:00," then *that* is a fact. You know that to be true. However, there is no guarantee the meeting will occur.

How about this statement: "I have an open requisition for a new hire, and I've seen 15 résumés." If true, that is a fact. It doesn't mean you'll hire anyone or that the requisition will remain open. It also doesn't mean you've reviewed the résumés; you may have just *seen* them.

What about this statement: "A customer called and said he is unhappy about the new policy described in the letter he received from my company." If you define a customer as someone who has purchased something from your company, and the person who called indeed purchased something from your company, then it would be a fact that you have a customer. It is a fact your company sent out a letter explaining a new policy on renewal fees. It is a fact the customer called and *said* he was unhappy. But is he really unhappy? Maybe he is just saying that to get a better rate. Maybe his unhappiness might really be disappointment, or maybe he is distraught. It is a fact that he claimed to be unhappy, but you cannot say it's a fact he is actually unhappy. There's too much wiggle room around all the possible definitions of *unhappy*. Remember, *if it generates a discussion—in this instance, just how unhappy is he?—then we don't call it a fact.*

Use *So What* with Facts

A handy clarity tool to use when someone claims to present facts is *so what*. Asking this question allows you to uncover the importance of the fact under consideration. Consider the statement about seeing 15 résumés; the *so what* here might be that it's hard to find a good candidate to hire, that you need to find another source for candidates, or that it's great news because you may have just opened the requisition yesterday.

Fact or Not Fact?

Let's take a look at the following facts and determine how factual they really are.

Fact: When we asked our customer how we could improve our service, he said, "Deliver your products in five days or less."

What's the fact here? Direct quotes from customers are facts, but the quote is the factual part, not necessarily the meaning behind it. The customer said we should deliver the product in five days or less, yet he might be satisfied with six days.

■ ■ ■

Fact: "It is raining outside."

I know this to be true, because I'm standing outside, it is raining on me, and I'm getting wet. "It is raining" is a fact.

■ ■ ■

Fact: "It currently takes us an average of about 2 hours to complete this task."

If the data are correct, this would be a fact.

■ ■ ■

Fact: "If we get this contract, we'll need to hire five people."

This is *not* a fact, because it's something that's taking place in the future. You might find that you will need to hire five people, but maybe you won't. Maybe you'll find the right person who can do the work of two. Maybe someone will quit, and you'll need to hire six.

■ ■ ■

Fact: "Some people are not great communicators."

Fact or not? We all know this is true based on our own idea of what communicating well entails. We've all met people whom we would describe as not being great communicators. Therefore, is this a fact? Is this absolutely true—does it generate discussion and debate? One question that might come about is "What do you mean by *great communicator*?" Until we define *great communicator*, this cannot be a fact.

The Takeaway

Facts are a component of your premise and are absolute truth. There are not many facts. Future events and predictions cannot be facts. Facts are not debatable. A fact is not "highly likely"; it is 100 percent, a sure thing.

If it's not a fact, then what is it? That's where observations come in.

17 Observations

Observations Are Abundant

We covered the first premise component, facts, in the last chapter. The next premise component is observation. *Observations* consist of all we read and what we hear. We don't know observations to be absolutely true, and we haven't personally experienced them. If an observation were absolutely true, it would be a fact. When you ask someone a question, the response is your observation—most of the time.

When you read in the morning news about some daredevil riding a motorcycle over a gazillion school buses, you're making an observation. You don't know for certain he jumped those buses. If the story comes from a reliable source, it *probably* is true; but you can't be certain of that, and if you were not there, you didn't witness it.

Here are examples of observations:

- You read a review of a restaurant on TripAdvisor.
- You're in a product-quality review meeting, reading a report that claims that customer satisfaction is at 72 percent. You don't know where the data came from, how accurate it is, or even what the customer was rating. This statement would generate a conversation, so it's an observation.
- A weather forecaster says, "It's going to rain tomorrow."
- Anderson Cooper on Cable News Network (CNN) says, "The president signed a new tax bill."

Why are these observations? You don't know them to be absolutely true.

There is much confusion between facts and observations. A statement coming from a trusted source carries great weight and can easily be counted as a fact (Why would that person lie or make it up?), despite the statement being only an observation. The added weight given based on a source's reliability makes your premise component seem strong.

For example, we tend to have more faith in a statement if a close friend or relative tells us something, as opposed to just hearing it from a casual acquaintance. The source doesn't have to be a person; it could be a database, a newspaper, or the Internet. Perhaps you hear someone say, "The Earth will be impacted by an asteroid 20 miles across within the next 10 years." You ask that person, "Where did you get that information?" and he or she replies, "I read it on the Internet at a doomsday website." You probably would not put much stock in that statement, because you recognize the weak source of information. However, if a noted astronomer said that same thing and substantiated it with observations from his or her telescope, you'd best be looking for an underground shelter.

Despite all the confusion, distinguishing facts from observations is simple. It's a fact if you can say yes to the following question: "Is this information absolutely true, with no question, no discussion, no explanation, and no variation?" If your answer is no, and you have never experienced this event before, then it's an observation. Observations have the *possibility of being true or untrue.*

Observations require conversations and understanding of how accurate they are or under what circumstances they are true. Someone says, "Our customers want faster service." Sounds like a fact, but some customers may want higher quality over faster service. It's worth having the conversation to get clear.

Suppose you say, "I own a home." If you have a mortgage, then technically both you and your bank own the home. A conversation would occur about how much you owe. It's an observation.

Perhaps your boss says, "Our employees are motivated." This might be the overwhelming attitude. But there may be some who are not, or there are circumstances under which they would not be. Having a conversation about those employees and circumstances will help in understanding a situation. It's an observation.

Maybe a politician says, "We have cut $10 million of spending this year." The truth might be that although $10 million was cut,

$8 million was added, so the net reduction was really $2 million. It's an observation.

Here is why it's important to distinguish observations from facts. We use facts and observations as part of our premise that leads to a conclusion for our headscratcher. Facts are black and white. Observations require additional clarity and conversation. Gaining clarity leads to a better understanding of some of the options you have to address a situation. If something happens often, you might do one thing, but if it happens rarely, you might do another. It's important to distinguish this. For example, you may say, "My chain on my bicycle always falls off." After a discussion, this may really mean, "My chain on my bicycle falls off many times when I'm changing the front gear and going up a steep hill." The conclusion you reach about how to fix this problem might be very different in these two circumstances.

When someone uses a term such as *always, never, none, all,* or *every,* eyebrows should rise. Statements that use these terms imply they are facts, yet often they are not. For example, "We always put the heavy equipment in that space over there." Perhaps there are circumstances that prevent you from using the usual space; *always* becomes *most of the time,* making this an observation. Using terms such as *always* and *never* shuts down conversations because there's nothing to talk about. If it's true, it's clear, but most of the time it really isn't absolute. Make it an observation and dig a little deeper to understand the circumstances.

The Takeaway

Observations are events, occurrences, and information we do not know to be absolutely true and have not experienced for ourselves. Even if something sounds like it's always true, or someone reliable has communicated that observation, it's merely an observation if you don't know it to be absolutely true. Although it may *be* true, it also may not be. Observations require conversations about the circumstances behind them. This understanding of circumstances leads to more precise solutions.

We'll be coming back to observations in Chapter 21, "The Conclusion: Putting It All Together." At this point, we've covered two premise components: facts and observations. Let's take a look at the next component.

Exercises to Distinguish Facts and Observations

Are These Facts or Observations?

1. You are reading this sentence now.

2. On the Earth, if you drop something, it will fall to the ground.

3. Windows are made from glass.

4. The economy is better now than it was in 2009.

5. My project is due in 45 days.

6. Successful businesses have innovative products.

7. My manager is responsible for evaluating performance.

8. As a manager, I'm responsible for evaluating the performance of my direct reports.

9. Our competitors just lowered their prices.

10. Over the past year, I received more than 50 e-mails per day.

Answers

1. Fact, unless someone is reading it to you; then it would be an observation.

2. Observation. You would think this is a fact, but if you drop a helium balloon, it will rise! If you said, "The Earth attracts objects due to gravity," this would be a fact as defined by our current understanding of science.

3. Observation. Are all windows glass? I don't know. If you don't know either, it's an observation.

4. Observation. Most would agree, but not if they're unemployed.

5. Observation. It may be a fact that it is on the calendar, but a lot of things could happen that would postpone the due date;

(continued)

(*continued*)

    therefore, it's an observation. If the statement were, "My project is scheduled to be completed in 45 days," that would be a fact.

6. Observation. Although this may be true, can there be successful companies that are not innovative? Many companies are very successful because they are operationally efficient, not because they are innovative.

7. Fact. If it's in your manager's job description that he or she is responsible for this, then it would be a fact. (It doesn't mean the manager will do it, but he or she is responsible for it.)

8. Fact. If it's in your job description, then it's a fact.

9. Observation. All of them or some of them? Temporarily or permanently?

10. Fact. I can't vouch for you, but this is definitely a fact for me! It doesn't mean I'll continue to receive over 50 e-mails per day as there could be a major communications outage, or just an unusually slow day, but for the past year I definitely received more than 50 e-mails per day. This is a fact for me, but it's only an observation for you because you don't know this is true— maybe I'm making it up (I wish!).

18 Experiences

Your Experiences

Experiences are probably the most valuable assets you have, because they are made up of all your actual firsthand involvements. If you were there, if it happened to you, or if you saw it—it's an experience.

Experiences can *only be from the past*. Although they are very real to you, remember, your brain makes things up, throws things out, and distorts things. Just because you had an experience doesn't mean your interpretation of it was the same as someone else's with the exact same experience. For example, two people can order the same meal at a restaurant. After leaving the restaurant, one person says, "That was a great meal and restaurant"; the other person says, "I didn't enjoy that, the meal was just so-so, and it was noisy in there."

Remember our discussion of emptying your bucket? Here's why it's so important to understand and be aware of what's in your bucket: the stuff in your bucket comes from your experiences, and experiences play a major role in how you come to conclusions. If you're not aware of your bucket's contents, then you're not aware of the experiences that lead you to a given conclusion. As a result, your breadth of conclusions is narrow. If you're aware and you can get rid of what's in your bucket—or at least ignore it for a little while—your breadth of conclusions is greatly enhanced. You'll be able to come up with new ideas you may have normally discarded. For example, suppose you had a prior interaction with someone who was not cooperative, and was perhaps even a little nasty. Your bucket has that experience in it, even though you don't know the circumstances behind that person's attitude. You now have a need for some information from that same person.

If your bucket isn't empty, you might approach that person with a very standoffish, matter-of-fact attitude and just say, "Can you please give me this information?" Instead, if you emptied your bucket, as if you had never had that prior interaction, you might approach this person and say, "Hi. I wonder if you might assist me? I have this project due next week, and I need this information. Can you please help me with this?" Your conclusion about how to ask this person for assistance is very different with an empty bucket. His or her cooperation might be, too.

Here are some examples to help you distinguish observations from experiences:

- Someone says to you, "It's raining outside." That's an observation.

- If you're standing outside in the rain, and you say, "It's raining outside," that's an experience.

- The nightly news reports the road you take to work will be under construction tomorrow. That's an observation.

- The newspaper in the morning says the road you take to work will be under construction today—another observation.

- You set out to work on the road you usually take, and you see the construction going on—that's an experience.

- A colleague tells you, "We're going to have a meeting tomorrow." This can't be a fact, because it's in the future and because you don't know it will actually happen. It can't be an experience, because it's in the future. Therefore, it's an observation.

To review:

- Facts are absolute truths.

- Observations *aren't* absolute truths, and you have not experienced them.

- Experiences are your firsthand encounters.

So What?

Let's turn the table, use a little critical thinking, and ask *so what:* That is, so what if it's a fact, an observation, or an experience? Why does that matter?

A fact is an absolute truth, so you can rely on it. A premise with facts in it can be very strong, making any conclusions based on that premise highly reliable.

Observations generally carry less weight than our own experiences. We tend to trust what we've witnessed ourselves more than what others claim, especially if we have personal experience. Observations generate discussion about how reliable they are. They can vary greatly, from wild fiction to highly probable truth. Experiences generate discussions about how frequent, relevant, and indicative to the headscratcher they are.

The Takeaway

Experiences are events where you have actually been there and done that or at least tried that or witnessed that. Your involvement doesn't mean you haven't distorted it somehow, but you have experienced it. The more experience you have with a particular issue, the stronger your premise will be. Experiences are great, but they do not stand alone in critical thinking—so beware of them.

In Chapter 21, "The Conclusion: Putting It All Together," we use and weigh these different components of the premise to reach a conclusion. In the meantime, hang in there, because there are two more premise components: beliefs and assumptions.

Exercises to Distinguish Facts, Observations, and Experiences

Are These Facts, Observations, or Experiences?

1. Someone says to you, "Wow, there's a lot of traffic out there."

2. You are driving and you say, "Wow, there's a lot of traffic out here."

(continued)

(*continued*)

3. You pass a road sign that says, "Traffic ahead."

4. Our projects are always late.

5. I just spoke to a customer. He said that our service is the best he has ever experienced.

6. The store's hours are posted, and the sign reads, "Open at 9:00 AM."

7. The store opens at 9:00 AM.

8. I went to the store, and the door was locked.

9. Our supplier said it will have the delivery to us within three days.

10. In the past, when our supplier says it will deliver within three days, I always see the delivery truck pull up in one or two days.

Answers

1. Fact and observation. It's a fact that he or she said it. It's an observation that there is traffic. What is traffic to him or her might be just minor congestion to you.

2. Experience. You're there. It's still not a fact that there is traffic, because that's a relative term, but from your perspective, there is traffic.

3. Fact and observation. It's a fact that the road sign says "Traffic ahead," but it's an observation, same as answer number one.

4. Observation. There's that *always* word. You don't know this to be true.

5. Experience and observation. You've experienced the conversation. What the customer told you is an observation.

6. Fact and observation. It's a fact that the hours posted say 9:00 AM and an observation that the store will really open at 9:00 AM.

   7. Observation. Says who?

   8. Experience. You were there. The door was locked.

   9. Observation. You don't know that.

  10. Experience. You were there. Here is an example of how you might distort things and why this wouldn't be a fact. The statement reads, "I always see . . ." Perhaps that is true; perhaps you think it's true, but you may have thrown out (forgotten) that one time they didn't arrive for four days.

19 Beliefs

Beliefs—Your Value System

At an international distance race in Spain in late 2012, Kenyan runner Abel Mutai was in first place, followed by Spaniard Ivan Fernandez Anaya. For some reason—perhaps the way the course was marked—Mutai thought the end of the race was about 10 meters before the actual finish line, and he slowed to a stop. The Spanish crowd attempted to point out the error, but Mutai didn't understand the foreign language. Anaya could have overtaken Mutai and claimed first place but instead came up behind him. He guided Mutai to the finish line, preserving the outcome as if Mutai had not made his mistake. When asked why he didn't overtake Mutai, Anaya explained that he wasn't the rightful winner and if it weren't for Mutai's confusion, he would have not won. The conclusion Anaya made—to help his competitor—was heavily influenced by a belief about doing the right thing.

We all have values. Many are shared; some are different. Not everyone has a strong do-the-right-thing value; some people have an every-man-for-himself value. Some people believe that their job takes priority over their personal life, whereas others feel the opposite. Some think it's perfectly acceptable to take a few office supplies home for personal use, but others consider it stealing and would never do so. Being on time is extremely important to some people; others think it's perfectly okay to be late. Regardless of the stance, these are all beliefs.

Beliefs are your core values. They are not statements such as "I believe we should do this!" or "My belief is that the project should be cancelled."

These are conclusions or tasks to do, not beliefs. Using the word *believe* about something doesn't automatically make that thing a belief. Beliefs are not situational; they don't vary with circumstances. They are about you and your values.

Many people assume that critical thinking is a nonemotional, objective process. Although that would be nice, it's impossible—because we are human. We have values that we apply to everything we do. The conclusions you reach will be consistent with your values. The thousands of conclusions you make daily are influenced by your values—what you believe to be right or wrong, good or bad, proper or not.

Here are a few examples:

- You're walking down the sidewalk, and you notice a wallet on the grass. You pick it up. There's about $200 in it and no identification. Should you keep it or turn it over to the police? Your choice depends on what your values are.

- You purchase something in the store labeled $19.99. The cashier rings up $9.99. Do you correct the mistake? It depends on your values.

- You're finishing up a project, and you notice an error in a 100-page document that's otherwise ready to go to print. The typo would have little to no effect and probably would not be noticed. Do you delay and fix it? What do your values say?

- You're having dinner with your family at a nice restaurant, and your 18-month-old child is upset about something and crying. Do you stay at the table, making failed attempts to stop the crying? Do you excuse yourself and carry your child out of the restaurant? It depends on your values.

We call these values your beliefs. They consist of your constitutional merits and flaws, including your prejudices. They're the same at work or at home, whether you're with family, friends, or strangers. And they're virtually the same as an adult as they were when you were a kid.

You use your beliefs as a filter or gate, and you make conclusions that are consistent with your filter. Some people have values about being non-confrontational, whereas others consider confrontation just fine—even necessary. Two people might come to very different conclusions in the same circumstances; one person may speak up, whereas one remains quiet. Some place value on following rules, whereas others believe rules were made to be broken.

Although you might disagree with someone's beliefs (values), you can't tell someone his or her values are wrong. Values are core to an individual, so telling someone his or hers are wrong falls on deaf ears. You can *respectfully disagree* with someone's beliefs, but that's about it. Consider the topic of religion. You may have a religion or you may not. But if you have a particular belief and tell others theirs are wrong—how are they likely to react? A more acceptable approach would clearly be to acknowledge their beliefs and simply have a different view.

Let's first take a look at where beliefs come from, the beliefs of the people you associate with, and then examine the important question about how to reconcile a disagreement if beliefs are different.

Beliefs are generally formed when you are very young and are heavily influenced by your environment. Let's say you and your family ate dinner together when you were a child, and your parents often talked about people who dyed their hair different colors—how unusual that was and how those people were irresponsible and poor workers. You grow up with a prejudice toward people who dye their hair different colors, despite your never having met a person with hair dyed different colors. Now you're all grown up, your manager comes to introduce you to your new work peer, and she has hair dyed a bright fluorescent green and blue. You freak out and say to your manager, "Oh my, we are in *so much* trouble. This person is going to be irresponsible and a bad worker."

Your manager says, "Why do you say that? She has an impeccable history of accomplishments."

"She has green and blue hair. People who dye their hair colors are bad workers," you say.

"Nonsense," your manager says, but you'll discount what your manager says, because your prejudice is part of who you are. You begrudgingly work with this person, and, to your surprise, she's okay. However, you're still not convinced.

The next person comes in, and he has bright yellow and red hair. "Oh, no, not again," you think. Your manager tells you everything will be all right. You work with this person, and he too is okay—actually, a very effective employee. Therefore, over time—possibly a long time—you'll be fine with people who have different colored hair. Your beliefs change based on experiences contrary to your values, but it takes awhile for this to happen. Your beliefs don't change because someone says, "You're nuts," "That's not right," or "Don't believe that."

There are 7 billion people in the world, but there aren't 7 billion values. It is no coincidence that you share beliefs with your friends and have a common set with your work associates. You would not befriend someone with different values. People who have values different from the office culture are generally unsuccessful in a given work environment. For example, say you work in the health care industry as a home health aide. More than likely, you have beliefs related to helping others, as do your peers. Now a new employee enters and says, "You know, people who are sick need to help themselves and not rely on healthy people." How long do you think that person would keep this job? Either the employee would be fired, or he or she would quit because he or she would be miserable working with that attitude. Most of the people you work with share values because if they didn't, they wouldn't fit in and would subsequently leave.

When Beliefs Are Different

Although the people we associate with usually have shared values, we do have some different values—and it's hard to change someone's beliefs, no matter how wrong you perceive them to be. How do you deal with people who disagree about a conclusion when their beliefs differ from yours? It's an important question although a less common issue in the business world than you think. Not only do we work with people who share many of our values, but also the weight you put on your values at work will typically be less than on highly personal issues. Beliefs have less influence on your professional conclusions than on your personal ones.

People usually disagree in a business setting about something because of varied facts, observations, and experiences. Nevertheless, there will be those times when a belief is where the disagreement mainly resides and obstructs a conclusion. For instance, you're collaborating with a peer who believes in doing things right the first time. You're working on a computer software project that you need to finish up. A passionate discussion ensues. You say, "Okay, our solution won't last forever, but I think we're good to go."

Someone else chimes in, "No, we're not ready. If we finish now, we'll just have to do it again someday. We need to do it right *this* time."

There is no right or wrong here; your values are simply different. Things escalate to your manager, who sides with finishing up now, and if there's something to redo down the road, so be it. If he or she thinks critically, your manager would say to your coworker, "I know you are all about doing it right the first time and there's merit to that. However, there is great benefit in this particular instance in getting this out the door now. I acknowledge that we might have to redo some things down the road, and if we delayed now we might avoid that; but I'm okay with having that exposure. So can you be okay this time?" It's a mouthful, but when you acknowledge someone's belief, you help him or her align with another conclusion. Of course, if you had that conversation every day, that person would probably quit at some point.

What happens if a person digs his or her heels in so deeply about a belief that he or she is immovable? This instance rarely occurs in business, but it can. This individual puts so much weight on a belief that he or she might discount or ignore facts, observations—even personal experiences. The matter becomes irreconcilable—and there is a big difference here between critical and automatic thinking. Irreconcilable differences in critical thinking are based solely on different fundamental values and are uncommon. But the differences we *think* are irreconcilable in automatic thinking are actually reconcilable, because they are based on dissimilar facts, observations, and experiences. What most likely could have been resolved is not, and misunderstanding and bad decisions from filled buckets are the result.

Belief-only disagreements are generally more prevalent in personal relationship and geopolitical worlds. It can be an interesting exercise to have a conversation with someone from an opposing political view about the economy, the government, or foreign policy. Beliefs will surface fast; you'll disagree and then see how challenging it is to reconcile those disagreements.

One question remains, however: Can you resolve a disagreement that is based solely on an immovable, unwavering, uncompromising, do-or-die belief? This is when words such as *irrational* come into play—and then there is no reconciliation. In business, the boss will make the call, and if some people are simply unable to digest the conclusion, then they quit. Unfortunately, the only way humans have found to reconcile these fundamentally opposing ideological beliefs in the geopolitical world is often through violence or war. Critical thinking *can* prevent most of this, because it will bring to the surface disagreements based on facts, observations, and experiences; however, it doesn't always work.

The Takeaway

We all have core values called beliefs, which are one of the components that comprise our premise. We apply our beliefs in the thousands of conclusions we reach each day. Understanding our beliefs doesn't remove emotion, but it allows us to recognize how they influence our conclusions—which gives us a more thoughtful perspective of those conclusions.

So far, we have covered facts, observations, experiences, and beliefs. There's one more component of our premise to cover: assumptions. Once we describe assumptions, we'll put all the premise components together, and you'll see how everything works.

20 Assumptions

Assumptions Are Key

You've probably been warned more than once in your life not to make assumptions. This advice is far from accurate; it's necessary to make assumptions. You can't come to a conclusion about anything without making assumptions.

An *assumption* is a thought you have and presume to be correct. Based on that, you can come to a conclusion. The big difference between automatic versus critical thinking is:

- In automatic mode, you take it for granted your assumptions are correct.

- In critical thinking mode, you ask, "How do I know my assumption is a good one?"

The advice about assumptions should be, "Don't make assumptions without knowing how you arrived there or make assumptions you cannot validate."

Have you ever left for work earlier than usual because the weather was bad and because you had to be there by a certain time? You assumed it would take longer to get to work because it was raining, snowing, or hailing. *Why* did you assume that? Because you've dealt with the situation before, and just about every time the weather is bad, the commute is slower. Therefore, your assumption is probably valid.

Let's say you're working on a project, and one team member you've never met is late to a status meeting. There is another status meeting one week later. Do you assume this member will be late? Because you've had only one experience with him or her, making that assumption would be a poor choice. However, if he or she were late to four out of the last five status meetings, then it would be a fair assumption to make.

Assumptions are formed from facts, observations, and experiences. You make an assumption about what might occur or what the current situation is. For example:

- It's 8:00 AM on Saturday morning. Your child has a soccer game scheduled at 2:00 PM (observation: although it's a fact that it is scheduled, there is no guarantee that it will actually occur). You hear the weather report: 90 percent chance of rain, starting at 11:00 AM and continuing through the rest of the day (observation). For the last three years, your kid's soccer game was cancelled when it rained (experience). Therefore, based on the starting time of the game (observation), the rain forecast (observation), and cancelled games because of rain (experience), you make the assumption this afternoon's soccer game will be cancelled.

- The last 10 times you had a conversation with your manager, you got more work to do (experience). You're in a situation where you need to have a conversation with your manager. You might rightly assume if you have this conversation with your manager, you'll probably get more work to do.

- A particular customer calls and places an order (fact). He cancelled the last six orders he placed (experience). You ask how firm the order is; he claims it's very firm (observation). You think to yourself, "That's what he said the last four times, and he *still* cancelled" (experience). Therefore, you figure you probably shouldn't count on this sale, because there's a good possibility he will cancel it (assumption).

You make thousands of assumptions each day, most of which you take for granted. When we drive our car to a store to buy something, we assume, among many other things:

1. We won't have a flat tire.
2. The car's gas gauge is correct.

3. The roads won't all be closed.

4. The store will be open.

5. We will be able to pay for the merchandise.

6. The store will have the merchandise.

We make a ton of assumptions, all based on facts, observations, and experiences.

Here is a more complicated example: You're attending a project status meeting to determine whether your group will complete this project on time. Most of the milestones look good and tasks are being accomplished, but a few are behind schedule. The people in charge of those deliverables say, "Yes, it's a yellow flag, but we think we'll be okay." Two days later, the same tasks now have red status because they have fallen *further* behind. Again, people assure you that things will be all right. You've found while working with these folks that they tend to be optimists with good intentions and work really hard, but they miss milestones. Based on this experience, you make the assumption the group will not finish the project on time.

If you make assumptions based on facts that are not *facts*, on observations not indicative of a situation, or solely on a single experience, then your eventual assumption might not be a good one. You go into a store and see an item you recognize at a very low price. Would it be correct to assume that the prices for other items are low? Of course not, because it's only one experience, in essence, one item. However, if you examined 30 recognizable items, and almost all were at a lower price than the store from where you usually buy, you could assume the prices at this store are lower—at least on that day.

We make countless assumptions in automatic mode. But in critical thinking, we don't take our assumptions for granted. We ask what facts, observations, and experiences we are using to come up with these assumptions. Can we validate or invalidate these assumptions by gathering additional observations? Do others have different, contrary experiences?

People make different assumptions because they have different observations or experiences. If you listened to a weather report that said there might be rain (observation) but your friend heard a different weather report, then you might assume you need to bring an umbrella, but your friend would not.

The Takeaway

We make thousands of assumptions each day, all based on facts, observations, and experiences. Some of these assumptions are poor, because they are based on weak premise components—maybe only one observation or an experience not representative of the current situation. In critical thinking, we ask, "Why am I making these assumptions? How do I know they are good ones? What facts, observations, and experiences am I using to form that assumption?"

Now it's time to put it all together. Facts, observations, experiences, beliefs, and assumptions comprise the premise. In the next chapter, we'll look at how these components are combined to form your solutions (conclusions) and how people combine them differently.

21 The Conclusion

Putting It All Together

*C*onclusions are solutions to our headscratchers. Recall the components we detailed in the prior chapters: facts, observations, experiences, beliefs, and assumptions. Collectively, these make up the premise. Now we'll put them together and see how they form a conclusion. Then we'll cover why some conclusions are more reliable than others and how to strengthen confidence in a conclusion. Finally, I'll explain how our personalities play a role in the conclusions we make and what to do when people have different conclusions than we do—how to resolve and agree.

This is a bigger chapter than the others, because conclusions are a big deal. They're what allow you to solve your headscratcher. Although clarity is the first step in critical thinking, and you can't solve a problem well without being clear about what that problem is, it's the conclusion that moves you from problem to solution.

Creating the Premise

We combine facts, observations, and experiences to form an assumption. Figure 21.1 shows how everything in this process relates.

In Figure 21.1, facts, observations, and experiences form the foundation for assumptions. That's why they are below *assumptions* in our visual; they *support* them. We then apply our belief filter to yield a conclusion and figure out what to do.

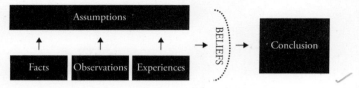

Figure 21.1 The Conclusion Process

Here are a few examples to show you the entire process.

Situation A: You have an important meeting tomorrow, and the weather looks bad.

- *Fact:* Water reduces friction between your car tires and the road.

- *Observation:* The 6:00 PM weather report says there will be a downpour during the morning rush hour.

- *Experience:* When it rains like crazy in the morning rush hour, traffic moves slowly. It takes longer to get to work; you've experienced this many times.

- *Assumption:* It's probably going to take longer to get to work tomorrow morning (based on the preceding facts, observations, and experiences).

- *Belief:* Being on time is important. I said I would be at the 8:00 AM meeting, so I will.

- *Conclusion:* I will set my alarm 30 minutes early so that I can get to my 8:00 AM meeting on time.

Situation B: A customer calls and is upset about being billed improperly.

- *Facts:* A customer calls and tells you he's upset. This individual has been a customer for nine years and always pays his bills on time.

- *Observation:* When you examine what you billed him, you see products listed that the customer claims he did not order.

- *Observation:* Peers tell you that they like helping this customer and that he buys a lot.

- *Experience:* In the nine years this person has been our customer, he has complained four other times about being billed for products he did not order. We found after investigating each incident that the customer was correct.

- *Experience:* We sometimes have this problem with our billing system.

- *Belief:* People should acknowledge their errors and not blame others.

- *Assumption:* This customer is probably right, because of experiences with both him and our billing system.

- *Conclusion:* Apologize for the error, and adjust the bill for the customer.

- *Conclusion:* Ask the billing department why or how this problem can occur and what we can do to prevent it from happening again.

Situation C: You have an opening for a new employee. You are interviewing and have identified three good candidates. You need to come to a conclusion about to whom to make an offer.

- *Fact:* Each candidate lives locally, is employed, and has more than 10 years of work experience.

- *Fact:* Candidate 1 got unanimous thumbs-up from the interview team, whereas candidates 2 and 3 got a thumbs-up from 9 out of 10 interviewers.

- *Fact:* The same person gave candidates 2 and 3 the thumbs-down, and the reason given was "not my personality type."

- *Fact:* Candidates 1 and 3 have asked for a salary slightly above the target.

- *Experience:* We don't always offer a salary based on what a candidate asks for.

- *Observation:* Candidate 1 arrived late for two out of the three interview appointments, blaming her tardiness on traffic.

- *Observation:* Candidates 1 and 2 both have résumés filled with impressive projects, but it's not clear what they did on those projects.

- *Observation:* References for all candidates checked out great. Candidate 3's references were glowing.

- *Experience:* Candidates generally provide references that give positive feedback.

- *Observation:* Candidates 1 and 2 have great experience in the specific job function sought and have spent most of their careers in that job function. Candidate 3 has less experience in the specific job function but has experience in several related job functions.

- *Experience:* If someone is successful in multiple jobs or responsibilities, that success shows he or she can adapt and apply skills in different areas.

- *Observation:* Candidates 2 and 3 say they are considering a few job offers.

- *Belief:* People can apply their skills anywhere.

- *Belief:* Being late for an important meeting shows poor planning.

- *Assumption:* We probably can't go wrong with any of these candidates.

- *Assumption:* Our company is going through changes, and we'll need to have flexible people on board who can handle different responsibilities.

- *Assumption:* Candidate 3 is diverse and successful, and her experiences demonstrate her ability to succeed in very different situations.

- *Conclusion:* Make an offer to candidate 3.

In situation C, the hiring manager put the most weight on the observation that candidate 3 was successful in many diverse job experiences and responsibilities. The hiring manager indicated he had multiple positive experiences with people who handled diverse job responsibilities.

The Stronger the Premise, the More Reliable the Conclusion—and the More Confidence You'll Have in It

The stronger the premise, the more confidence you'll have in your conclusion. Conversely, if your premise is weak, your confidence in your conclusion is lower. Consistent facts, observations, and experiences provide strong premise components, and strong premises contain assumptions that you can validate. Weak premises, on the other hand, have assumptions that you cannot validate—because they aren't supported by facts, observations, and experiences.

Here are a few examples of strong and weak premises:

- In situation A, if the weather report on one TV station was for a downpour, yet the Weather Channel predicted sunny and warm and an Internet weather forecast predicted a 30 percent possibility of widely scattered showers, then your premise would have contradictory observations. This yields a weak premise, and your conclusion about getting up early would be questionable. If all three sources confirmed that it would be pouring, your conclusion about getting up early would be a good one if you want to get to that meeting on time.

- In situation B, when you checked the customer's prior purchasing records, if you found that he once claimed he didn't order something but actually did (contrary observation), then you wouldn't be so quick to assume he was correct now. Your conclusion may have been to take a closer look at the shipping records (to validate or invalidate your assumption).

- In situation C, if one of the references for candidate 3 mentions how the candidate was unsuccessful in many of her different job responsibilities, the assumption about her being successful is invalid, thereby weakening the premise. Then the conclusion to hire candidate 3 becomes dubious. If the assumption is invalidated prior to offering the job, the hiring manager would change his mind or at least investigate further to completely invalidate (or revalidate) the assumption.

- In the pharmaceutical industry, a tremendous amount of research is conducted when a new drug is created. Experiments are performed that produce a mountain of data (facts, observations, and experiences). Assumptions are made from these data with respect to the drug's effectiveness, as well as possible side effects—and before the Food and Drug Administration (FDA) approves a drug, the pharmaceutical company must validate these assumptions. One of the ways companies do this is with extensive clinical trials—highly controlled and monitored human assessments. If the trials (experiences) prove that the drug assumptions are correct, the confidence in the conclusion—that the drug is okay—is high. However, if trial results contradict the assumptions, there will be low confidence in the conclusion—and the FDA will not approve the drug.

- You've invited a guest to your new house, and you expect to give a tour when he arrives. Having a very neat home is important to you (belief), so before his arrival, you ask your children to put the clothes on their bedroom floors in the laundry basket and to make their beds. Your kids are neat, so you assume they will do what you ask. Your guest arrives, and after a while, it's time for the tour. When you get to one child's bedroom, it's a mess, and you're embarrassed. In this case, the assumption that your children would do as you asked when you asked was a bad one. A bad assumption leads to a bad conclusion (in this case, thinking you can take your guest on a tour). If you had validated your assumption by peeking your head in your children's bedrooms before your tour, you would have realized the assumption was bad and postponed the tour (changed your conclusion) to avoid the embarrassment.

You must examine whether your premise is strong when reaching conclusions, and make sure your facts are *facts*! Have multiple observations and experiences that are consistent with each other. Make assumptions, but be sure to validate them.

Jumping to Conclusions

Every person moves from premises to conclusions thousands of times a day. You make conclusions about what to wear, what to eat, what to say, when to say it—everything you do. You conclude about your projects, your priorities, whether you are finished, what else you need to accomplish, and who needs to do what. You need the premise components first, and then a conclusion will follow.

At this point in our critical thinking workshops, someone usually asks, "But what *exactly* is the mechanism that moves you from the premise to the conclusion?" You have likely been told, "Don't jump to conclusions." This is another meritless expression. Nobody actually knows how you get from your premise to a conclusion. You make assumptions within your premise, apply your beliefs, and then at some point, an idea comes to you. There's a jump, a leap, an aha moment when an idea comes to you. In other words, you *always* jump to a conclusion. A big difference between automatic thinking and critical thinking is that when we jump to a conclusion in automatic thinking, we think we're done. When we do so in critical thinking, we *ask* how we reached that conclusion: Specifically, what assumptions are we making, and why are we making them?

We question the reasoning behind our conclusions during critical thinking. This generates great conversations about the premise components that lead to those assumptions. Those conversations create confident conclusions or help identify a weak premise. Good conclusions come from strong premises that we've vetted, reviewed, and discussed.

This brings up an important point. The equation of facts, observations, experiences, beliefs, and assumptions that yields conclusions is *bidirectional*—meaning you can use this process in two ways. Starting with a clear headscratcher, you might say, "I don't know what I should do here, so I'm going to look at facts, observations, experiences, beliefs, and assumptions to help me." The second way is to think, "I have some ideas about what to do, so I'm going to ask myself: What assumptions am I making, and what facts, observations, and experiences am I using to make those assumptions? What beliefs may I be applying? Let's see if my premise is strong and supports those conclusions."

In other words, whenever you have an idea to solve a headscratcher, go ahead and jump to a conclusion—but then go back and ask, "What assumptions am I making and why?"

Where Do Personalities Fit In?

Our personalities play an important role in the conclusions we make. Everyone uses the same thinking process: inductive reasoning to reach a conclusion. However, we don't all *weigh* premise components the same. Some people put more weight on facts, others perhaps on their experiences or beliefs. Individual-specific weighting preferences mean that people can have the same information yet make different conclusions.

Here's a simple example. You, your spouse, and your child visit a car dealer, and you all see the same car. You all read the fact sheet about the size of the engine, horsepower, and automatic this and that. You all get a copy of *Consumer Reports* on the vehicle (observations). You take a test drive together (experience). Of course, safety for the family is important (belief). What happens? You observe the report indicating maintenance costs on the vehicle are high; you make the assumption it's expensive to maintain the car. Although safety is important to you, it is critical to your spouse. The report's safety ratings lead her to assume the car is very safe. Your child really likes the built-in USB port in the backseat (observations) and assumes this would be a really cool car in which to ride. You conclude the car isn't for you because the maintenance costs are too high. Your spouse decides the car is great because of the safety record, and your child insists this is the only car in existence because she can recharge her smartphone in it.

You form three conclusions based on how each of you weighed the premise components. You ultimately resolve this not by arguing about who's right or wrong but by discussing the premise components and why you weigh some more than others. For example, you explain to your child the other four cars you are considering also have USB ports in the backseat, causing you to weigh that observation less.

Very analytic people weigh facts very heavily. Some people will have an experience only once and weight it very heavily. (Ever have food poisoning at a restaurant? Ever been back there?) Our personalities influence our inductive reasoning and our premises. We all use the same process to think—but we weigh premise components differently, which results in different conclusions.

Which Conclusion Is Right?

Why do two people who have the same facts reach different conclusions? One reason might be that they have different observations or experiences. One person heard the weather report, and another missed it; as a result, one concludes to bring an umbrella, and the other does not. We have different beliefs, and these alter our premises. We have different experiences, which cause different premises. Even when we have the same facts, observations, and experiences, and we share the same beliefs, we weigh them all differently. Mixed assumptions result, leading to diverse conclusions. How do we reconcile different conclusions? Which one is right?

First, we need to accept that it isn't about right or wrong; it's about the confidence and probability of the conclusions with respect to being a *good headscratcher solution*. The question shouldn't be whose conclusion is right but what conclusion is *most beneficial* to the specific headscratcher. Here's a situation: you and your peer are working on a problem, and you say, "I think we should do this," but your peer says, "I think we should do that." Now is the time to be in critical thinking mode.

Don't argue about who is right or wrong. Start the conversation with, "We have a situation, and we have two conclusions. One of these conclusions is more optimal than the other in this exact situation, or perhaps neither is good, and there's another, better option. Our job is to determine the best solution for this situation. So, what assumptions are we making, and why are we making them?"

Here's a specific example. Joe and Lisa are project leads on a process improvement team. The team is finishing up a project that required a testing cycle. Lisa says, "We have tested enough. We are done."

Joe says, "We haven't tested enough. We are not done."

Lisa replies, "We have tested the same amount that we tested in prior process improvement initiatives, so I really think we are done now."

Joe stands his ground and says, "I know that we've tested the same, but we really need to test more."

Bruce, another project lead, steps in and says, "Hmm, we have two views here (conclusions). One may be more advised then the other, so Joe, why do you think we need to continue to test; what assumptions are you making?"

Joe responds, "I'm assuming that because we reworked a critical component only last week, we need to test at least that component several more times."

Lisa asks, "Joe, why do you think we reworked that critical component?"

Joe replies, "I read the e-mail that said that was going to happen."

Lisa says, "Oh. That didn't happen. We found a minor problem elsewhere and fixed it, retested many times, and we're good."

Joe nods and says, "Oh, in that case, I agree we have done enough testing. We're done."

In the previous example, because Joe had an observation that was inaccurate, his assumption was invalid, leading him to a conclusion that was not optimal. With a conversation about the premise components, that was cleared up easily and quickly.

Have a conversation about assumptions to uncover why each of you is making them. Go there first, because it will lead to a discussion about facts, observations, and experiences. Listen to animated people who say things such as "Because it's the right thing to do," "Because we are a leader in this space," or "Because we said we would do it." These are beliefs coming out. When you understand the premises, you now have something to discuss.

For example, you say, "I think we should make 1,000 units."

Someone else says, "No, no, make just 500."

You ask, "Why 500? What are your assumptions behind only 500?"

He says it's because we don't need that many, so you ask why.

"Because last week we sold only 750 (experience), and we have 250 leftover (fact). We'll probably only sell 750 this week (assumption), so we'll have enough."

You say, "Did you know marketing was rolling out a promotion? (Observation.) I'm assuming the demand for the product will be higher, and we'll need more on hand."

He says, "Oh, I didn't know that (missing observation). Given this new information (which changed the premise), we'll probably sell more (new assumption), so I agree—we should make 1,000 units (agreed-upon conclusion)."

You must have a premise conversation to reconcile different conclusions. Start by determining what assumptions everyone is making and why. These conversations are very productive, because they don't take long to uncover the differences in people's premise components that are leading to conflicting conclusions. Once revealed, you can have a fruitful conversation that will generally result in quick agreement.

Getting Started with *Conclusions*

You make thousands of conclusions a day. Many take only a second or two, and you're good at making them in automatic mode. When should you use critical thinking for conclusions?

In two very specific situations:

- You don't know what to do and have to figure it out.

- You already have a solution for your important headscratcher—and because the outcome makes a difference, you want to be confident in the conclusion.

If you are riding a bus and conclude to sit on the right side instead of the left side, the outcome doesn't really matter, and you should stay in automatic mode. However, if you choose to run a price promotion, release a new product, institute a new policy, or hire a new employee—those are conclusions that make a huge difference in your business. Using critical thinking for these situations certainly is warranted.

Here are a few other examples of times when you'll want to use critical thinking to arrive at a conclusion:

- *When someone says, "What should we do?" or you say, "What should I do?":* Start by listing some of the facts, observations, and experiences, and then ask, "What assumptions can we make from these?"

- *When you're given requirements for a deliverable:* Of course, you'll get clear on those requirements, but you'll also want to question the assumptions behind them. For example, is the manager assuming customers want a specific function because he or she talked with a number of them, or is he or she using a single e-mail request from one customer to decide upon this requirement?

- *When you hear someone say, "I assume . . .":* Don't say, "Don't assume." Ask supportively, "May I ask a question about that assumption? Why are you assuming that?" You're looking to have a fact, observation, and experience conversation. How strong is that assumption, and can this person validate it?

- *When you hear "I don't think that's a good idea," or "How about this idea?":* Start the conversation with, "We have two conclusions. One may be more appropriate for this situation than the other, so let's see what our assumptions are and how we got to them."

- *When you find yourself disagreeing with someone else's idea:* You can have the same conversation as directly above. Alternatively, ask yourself even before you have that conversation, "Gee, what assumptions could that person possibly have that would lead him or her to that conclusion?" You'll want to examine your own assumptions for strength and validity as well.

- *When you are negotiating:* Understand your assumptions prior to negotiating. Anyone with whom you're negotiating is using the same thinking process as you, so ask yourself, "What do I think the opposing party's assumptions are? Why?"

- *When you have to correct someone:* Think from the perspective of the person with whom you are speaking. He or she came to a conclusion using facts, observations, and experiences. He or she made assumptions and applied beliefs to reach a conclusion. If the person made an error, it is most likely an accident because of a bad assumption. Perhaps he or she relied on an experience not representative of the norm, read (observed) a memo wrong, or thought something was a fact when it was not. When you understand the premise used, you can focus on correcting the premise. He or she will not only see where the error occurred but also will learn from the mistake.

- *When being a thinking coach:* Use this technique when you're helping others figure out what to do. Remember: Don't tell your conclusion. Just stay with their premises by asking questions such as "What experiences have you had related to this issue?" or "What have you read, been told, or heard about this?" or "Based on the experiences, observations, and facts you've told me, what assumptions might you make? Is there a way to validate those?"

- *When involved in postproject analyses, lessons learned, or postmortems:* After you finish a project, review what went well, what didn't, and what lessons you learned. Use critical thinking to ask questions such as "What was our thinking behind this? What assumptions did we make and why? Did we validate those assumptions? If so, how? If not, why not? What lessons can we learn about the premise?"

The Takeaway

It's all about the premise and its components, which form conclusions. The stronger the premise, the more probable your conclusion, and the more confidence you'll have in that conclusion. The weaker the premise, the less probable it will be, and the less confidence you'll have. Conclusion tools are bidirectional. If you don't know what to do, start with the premise components, and make assumptions. Conclusions will come. If you've already come to some conclusions, ask how you got there. Start with the questions "What assumptions am I making?" and "Why am I making those assumptions?"

Exercises for Conclusions

Although you normally wouldn't use conclusion tools for simple, automatic conclusions, I'll suggest a few here so that you can practice:

1. Listen to any conversation between two people expressing their opinions, keeping in mind that an opinion is a conclusion. Listen carefully to what they say. You'll hear them convey observations as facts and talk about experiences. Although they might not say outright, "Here are my assumptions," you'll hear those come out, too.

2. As you think about your next lunch, think about how you actually conclude what to eat or where to go—whether you make lunch at home and bring it to work, go to the company cafeteria, or go out to eat. For example, it's Friday, you like hamburgers, and you see a special on juicy hamburgers in the cafeteria. You say, "That looks good (observation), but I haven't barbequed for a few weeks (experience). I think we'll grill this weekend (assumption), so maybe I should have the salad." You also considered what you read (observation) about too much cholesterol and how you don't feel great (experience) when you eat too many hamburgers and concluded that the salad is healthier for you. You'll be amazed how much thinking you do in automatic mode and how quickly you do it.

3. Try having an assumptions conversation about something you have already completed by asking how you accomplished it. Start by asking what assumptions you made when you began the task.

Because we've revealed how people conclude and the importance of the premise in that process, we can now take a look at how this process affects credibility, change, and influencing and persuading others. After that we'll visit the exciting world of innovation—reaching conclusions beyond your everyday thinking.

22 Credibility

How Credible Is the Premise?

You receive an unsolicited e-mail from Dr. Samuel Jones III, who says he is a noted attorney from some country you've never heard of. The e-mail reads, "The late King of the eastern region has died and bequeathed to you $50 million. For me to send you this money, please send me your social security number, with two credit card numbers (don't forget the three-digit CCV code on the back). Looking forward to your response."

Most people would conclude this is a bogus e-mail and delete it. They do so because the premise's observations have almost no credibility. Their brains say, "What's the probability that *any* of these observations is true?" Much has been written about these schemes and credit card fraud, so they assume that this is one of those scams and delete the e-mail.

On the other hand, you might be listening to the radio, and the emergency broadcast system interrupts and warns of a tornado in your county. You look outside at some menacing clouds, so you conclude that you should head to the basement. Why? Well, the emergency broadcast system isn't used to spread rumors, and it says a tornado was spotted (observation); you see menacing clouds outside—an experience that gives credibility to the alert—and you have multiple observations from tornado stories. These components lead you to assume a tornado is probable, so you hightail it to your basement.

You can see how important premise credibility is.

Credibility of Facts and Observations

Credibility relates to facts and observations; you usually presume
your experiences are credible because you've experienced them. When
determining whether facts and observations are credible, we ask if
they are:

- *Feasible and realistic:* Is what you're reading or being told feasible? Is it
  realistic? Yes, these are judgment calls, but they strengthen the premise
  from *your* perspective. Someone tells you that the company just broke
  its record for sales (feasible). You get an e-mail saying you just won $50
  million (not realistic).

- *Consistent with your knowledge:* Is what you are now observing consistent with your prior experiences or observations? You happen to know
  that a project is behind schedule, yet someone says everything is on
  schedule.

- *Received from a reliable source:* Information from a credible source is
  more likely to be true; of course, even credible sources can have misinformation. Which source would you give more credence, Gossip.com or
  CNN.com?

- *Verifiable:* Most important—yet often difficult to do—is to verify the
  information. Can you experiment, find another source, or in some way
  independently validate the observation or fact? Someone suggests that
  customers would be unhappy if you made a certain change. To verify
  this, you might hold a focus group or survey customers.

Why Do People Lose Credibility?

You've likely been told at one time or another that a certain person or organization has little credibility. This really means that this person's or group's
facts and observations are unreliable, contradictory to what we know to be
true, and unverifiable; therefore, we cannot trust the assumptions or
any subsequent conclusions this person or group makes. Once you lose

credibility, it's difficult to get it back, because people's buckets fill with a memory of your misinformation. You can avoid this by making sure your facts are *facts* and your observations are *credible*.

Getting Started with *Credibility*

Here are statements or situations when it would be wise to take a look at their credibility:

- When you are presented with facts or observations, ask yourself how credible the information is—and *why you think that*. Is there a way to increase the information's credibility—perhaps through another source, your own research, or something you can experience?

- When someone says, "Here are the facts," ask, "How do you know that to be true?"

- When someone says, "Here's the data," ask, "How was this data validated?"

- When someone says, "Here's my assumption," ask, "How did you come to that assumption?"

- When you read something, ask, "Does this sound credible? Could it happen? Is there another source? Is this source credible? Does this make sense?

The Takeaway

Are the facts and observations presented credible? If in doubt, testing observations and validating facts will raise the credibility and, in turn, strengthen your premise and raise confidence in a conclusion.

Exercises for Credibility

1. Determine whether this statement is credible: there are more atoms in the head of a pin than there are grains of sand on all the beaches of the world.

2. Which scenario would give you more confidence about receiving your order?

   a. I called my supplier, and they said they shipped my order.

   b. I called my supplier, and they said they shipped my order, and gave me the tracking number.

3. Spam filters often look at e-mail content and apply rules for credibility. Act as your own spam filter. Use the philosophy "If it's too good to be true, it probably is." Don't assume it's *definitely* bad, but use more scrutiny when deciding.

4. Look at a forecast, project, production schedule, or some plan with respect to completing something within a certain time frame. How realistic is the schedule? What observations give you confidence in that timeline? What can you do to raise confidence? What assumptions are you making about the schedule, and why?

23 Consistency

The Consistency of Your Premise Components

Another tool that ensures a strong premise is *consistency*, which is the way that premise elements support each other. For example, let's say you read glowing reviews for a restaurant on several review websites—dozens of them, and all were great. A few of your friends also ate at the restaurant and loved it too, and the American Automobile Association (AAA) rated it high. A newspaper article on the place rated it top-notch. The restaurant has been in business for 23 years. These observations are very consistent and would make you confident the restaurant is good. Then you read one review from a person who hated the place and said the service was slow, the food was cold, and the server was nasty. This review is inconsistent with everything else—but because there are so many positive reviews against the one negative review, you probably would discount it.

Premises are stronger when their components are consistent. However, inconsistency isn't necessarily a bad thing; it identifies conflicting information, which yields a suspicious, weak premise. When you understand why there's conflicting information, or if you can resolve the inconsistency, your premise becomes stronger. Let's say you're shopping online at Amazon.com. You're looking for an item you usually buy for around $20. Most of the items you observe online are also in the $20 range, but you see one for $14. Because that price is inconsistent with your experience and other observations, it catches your attention. You think about two possible conclusions:

either it's a great deal, or it's too good to be true. Your premise needs something to resolve this inconsistency, in this case, more observations. You might read some reviews on the vendor from others who purchased at that price or read the fine print to find out more details. Ultimately, you might find supporting evidence (observations) consistent with it being a great deal, so you buy it.

Consistency with your own experiences is a heavily weighted factor. If you hear about observations *inconsistent* with your experience, you'll discount those observations. For example, if you had a great experience with a customer support center for a product you purchased, you would tend to discount a statement from someone who said that company had awful customer support. You must take care here; again, we can distort things, so just because we've had the experience doesn't mean our memory is really the way things were. For example, if you played a solo clarinet piece during a band performance, you might think your performance was awful, yet others tell you it was great. You'll discount those observations because you have a distorted view of your performance. Also, we may have had too few experiences upon which we're putting too much unwarranted weight. Still, a warning light should flash. There's an inconsistency, so additional inquiries and review should be the next step.

Inconsistency in your premise is a signal that you are not done. If you can't explain why there are conflicting facts, observations, and experiences, then your premise is weak. Your subsequent assumptions will be suspect, as will the resulting conclusions. You must resolve any inconsistency.

For example, you're looking at a project schedule and everything is green—good to go and on schedule. When you ask team members, they say, "We have our challenges here, like we do every project; but things are looking good." You notice a number of people on the project are working very late each night, the department's stress level seems high, and people are postponing vacations. There's inconsistency with everything looking good and people working so hard. Although this might be the result of a dedicated team ensuring the project is finished on time, it could mean you are right at the edge of a problem. Would you take this information to your senior management and say, "The project is on schedule, and everything is good to go"—or would you first check out how close things are between "looking good" and "So far so good; but we're barely making every deliverable, and we're in big trouble if something unexpected happens"?

Getting Started with *Consistency*

Here are a few instances in which you want to take a close look at consistency:

- *When you are presented facts and observations:* Compare them with other facts, observations, and your experience. Are things consistent? Do they add up?

- *When reviewing data:* Is the data you're reviewing consistent? Let's say you're in a seasonal business; for example, you sell gardening tools. Every spring, you see a spike in demand for your product, but you're seeing less of that this year. You need to investigate this inconsistency.

- *When saying and doing:* Is what people are saying consistent with what they are doing? You may have heard the expression "Walk the talk." If you say, "We're all about the customer," but then do things that are *not* in the customers' best interest, your premise supporting the conclusion "We are customer-centric" would be suspect. For example, a customer calls with a problem at 4:50 PM, and your live support closes at 5:00. After 10 minutes of working with the customer, the support rep says, "I'm sorry; we are closing now. Please call us back tomorrow." How consistent do you think that customer will think you are with your brochure that says, "Customers are our number one priority, and we go the extra length to satisfy you"?

- *When observing trends:* Look for inconsistent events relative to a trend. For example, let's say you have a punctual employee. Suddenly, he or she is late often. This would be a reason to raise an eyebrow and investigate. Is there a personal issue? Is he or she looking for a job elsewhere?

- *When evaluating assumptions:* Facts, observations, and experiences should support and be consistent with an assumption when you ask yourself or others, "How did you arrive at that assumption?"

The Takeaway

Look for consistency in the premise. Are all observations consistent with each other? Are observations and facts consistent with your experience? Are you making assumptions consistent with the premise components?

Exercises for Consistency

1. What's a nice restaurant you remember visiting? Look up the reviews of that restaurant on TripAdvisor. Are those reviews consistent with your experience?

2. Retailer Wal-Mart's slogan advertises that they have "Always low prices" (an observation). Visit a Wal-Mart near you. Are the prices you see (now an experience) consistent with that statement? Look up another company's slogan, such as Subway's ("Eat fresh"). Is your experience consistent with that slogan? Now take a look at the company you work for. Are your products, services, customer treatment, and pricing all consistent with your company's slogan or advertisements?

3. Review some data related to your job reflecting a future outcome. If you're in sales or marketing, look at a forecast or a quota. If you're in development or on a project, use a project schedule; if you're in manufacturing, use a production forecast; in human resources, perhaps an employee attrition forecast; in finance, a financial forecast. Is the forecast (observation) consistent with the current trend, sales, revenue, project plan, or attrition rate? If so, you can have good confidence in the forecast. If not, maybe put this book down for a few minutes and find out *why!*

24 Triangular Thinking

Estimating the Unknown

Triangulation is a technique land and property surveyors use to measure distances to hard-to-reach objects indirectly. For instance, the Greek philosopher Thales used a form of triangulation to measure the heights of the pyramids. The first step is to measure two angles to some distant object, and then calculate the distance between the two points at which you measured the angles. You then use trigonometry to determine the distance to the faraway object without direct measurement.

Life can often present hard-to-reach solutions, too. Sometimes you're asked to provide an answer that you can't directly measure or obtain—for instance, how long something will take. Because that's a question about the future, you can estimate it—but you cannot give a definitive answer.

Another example is a medical syndrome diagnosis, such as Reye's syndrome, Tourette syndrome (TS), and irritable bowel syndrome (IBS)—all of which end in *syndrome*. This term is used to describe illnesses with no clear cause—just symptoms. These are sometimes hard to diagnose, because there are often no direct tests to determine whether someone has them.

One method for determining a high-confidence conclusion about what is going on or what to do in these situations is by using something we call *triangular thinking*. This approach requires that you view or measure the problem

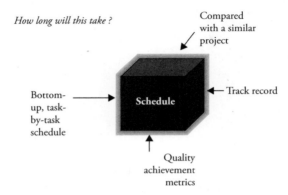

Figure 24.1 Estimating a Schedule with Multiple Perspectives

from several perspectives. Doing so produces a set of answers that you use to look for commonality or divergence. If all the views produce the same (or a similar) result, then you have a reliable answer (conclusion). On the other hand, if some views produce the same answer but others do not, then you don't have a clear understanding of the situation. In other words, triangular thinking is looking at the same problem but using different perspectives.

Figure 24.1 demonstrates triangular thinking by looking at the question "How long will it take to complete this particular project?" Because the schedule is a prediction of the future, you can't be 100 percent certain of your estimate. However, you want to have high confidence, so you look at the schedule from a few different perspectives, each of which is represented by a side of the cube. The first view might be to look at a bottom-up, task-by-task schedule, something that tells you that "This step will take 1 hour, this other piece 2 hours, this third piece 4 hours"—and so on. Once you add this all up, you have one answer. Another view is to consider your team's track record with respect to meeting deadlines. If it has a record of meeting initial estimates, then that's another data point. You might also compare this to other projects of similar size and complexity. A fourth view could be to track a quality metric, such as defects found in testing, as a predictor of the completion time.

Each of these methods yields an estimate. If all the estimates point to the same result, then you generate confidence in the answer. On the other hand, if triangular thinking produces different results, then something is not understood—and you're not able to provide a high-confidence estimate. If the bottom-up view produced a schedule of four months, yet several similar prior projects took eight months, then you'll need to conduct further review.

Similarly, you can use triangular thinking when asked to create a sales forecast to predict what you'll sell in the future. One perspective to include is the customers', considering what *they* are forecasting and planning. That gives you one estimate. Another might be based on track record. You review the previous eight quarters and see what percentage of the previous quarters' estimates were actually met. Last, you might take into account seasonality or new product releases to come up with a third view. Collectively, these will point to a forecast number that you think you'll be able to meet with confidence. If, however, the results of these perspectives are very different, then you have to take a closer look and ask, "Why?" Are the customers being overly optimistic or pessimistic? Is there something different about this quarter than previous quarters?

As you read in the forecast example, triangular thinking can be valuable in two ways. It can provide confidence in a conclusion that you might not normally be sure about or raise an alert that needs reviewing because information that should be consistent isn't.

Here's a memorable example of my use of triangular thinking—one that I used when my daughter was trying to decide to what colleges to apply. I took out a notepad, drew a cube (like the one in Figure 24.1), and said, "The answer is in this black box. You can't see inside, and won't really *know* if you have chosen the right answer until after you have applied, been accepted, and attended the school." She responded, "Dad, that's not much help!"

Without mentioning triangular thinking—or telling her where I thought she should apply—I continued. I explained that one way to look at the box was from the perspective of academics. Did the college have the academic program to fit her interest? Another perspective was travel time. How long would it take her to get to college or home again? (Of course, I was making the assumption she would want to come home occasionally!)

Activities were another viewpoint. Did the college have a swim club or marching band? What about a perspective concerning the opinions of others—her parents, her teachers, or the school's alumni? Yet another perspective might be to experience a visit. I drew the diagram with multiple arrows from different directions, all pointing to the box. She listened—at least I think she did. I told her when all the arrows point to the same answer or set of answers, then that's her answer. It was up to her what perspectives to use and how to weight the importance of each. She tacked the diagram to her bulletin board, where it still is today.

Although you can use triangular thinking to conclude or gain confidence in a conclusion, what I particularly like about this approach is its ability to *raise a flag* when something is amiss. When you view a situation from different perspectives, and the results are contradictory, it begs the question—Why? What is misunderstood? If a bottom-up schedule estimate is significantly different from similar projects' schedules, you have to ask yourself the reason for this. Is *this* project so much different? Are we concerned about something? Are we being overly optimistic if we think it will take a shorter time or pessimistic if we think it will take a longer time? When triangular thinking results in different answers, it *requires* you to investigate and understand.

Getting Started with *Triangular Thinking*

Here are a few places you should try out triangular thinking to ask yourself, Do multiple perspectives point to the same answer? If not, why not?

- *When you are asked for a schedule or forecast:* Use the example in Figure 24.1—consider bottom-up schedule, track record, and similar projects. Are these estimates all consistent? If not, why not?

- *When you're looking to find a root cause:* Triangulate on the evidence. What can cause each observation? What causes are common across all observations?

- *When you're making a prediction based on current trends:* Do all the trends support the same prediction?

The Takeaway

You can't know the future but can often provide a high-confidence estimate as to what will happen. To gain confidence in an answer, triangulate using multiple perspectives or indirect measures. If all views have similar results, then confidence in the answer is high. If there are different results, it's a flag. There's something misunderstood about the situation; go find out what.

Exercises for Triangular Thinking

1. Find five different sources on the Internet examining the Loch Ness Monster. On what explanation do they triangulate?

2. How many, and what, sources of news do you need to have confidence in a story?

3. Check the weather report for next week from four different sources: the local news, The Weather Channel, the National Weather Service (www.weather.gov), and the Farmers' Almanac. Do they triangulate on the same prediction?

4. Suppose your child came to you and asked:

   "How do I decide what sport to play?"

   or

   "How do I decide what club to join?"

   or

   "What instrument should I play?"

   What perspectives might you use to triangulate on an answer?

25 Change

The Premise and Change

One of the most challenging aspects of managing people is helping them through change—in their job, throughout an organization, or just with a project. By understanding how people reach conclusions, we can explain why people are uncomfortable with change and suggest ways to help people through change.

In order to explain the thinking that takes place during change, we have to look at the *premise* that forms our conclusions. Remember the premise components and how they work: facts, observations, and experiences are combined to form assumptions, which are filtered by beliefs, until you come to a conclusion. The stronger the premise, the more confident you can be in the conclusion; the weaker the premise, the less confidence you'll have. In the context of change, the conclusion is what to do—the actions that you or someone else should take. If you don't have confidence in this, you'll be uneasy about taking those actions.

As you'll see in the examples that follow, you often lack experience when change occurs—experience in that new venture, process, or manager. When your experience diminishes, your premise weakens—and as we have seen, a weaker premise means less confidence in the conclusion. You're not sure about what to do or say or how to act. As a result, you feel uncomfortable with the change.

By way of example, let's say there is an organizational change taking place. You have a new manager, and your responsibilities are changing somewhat. What part of the premise has changed? Facts are still facts, because they are absolute and cannot change. Observations—what you read or have been told—could change a bit. But most of the change will be your experiences. You don't have any history with this new manager, or familiarity with your new job responsibilities. Perhaps you don't have knowledge of the applications you'll use in that new job. If you're in a new group, you don't have experience with the other members and their group dynamics.

You have less experience in the new environment than you had in the old environment, which causes your premise, supporting what you should do, to weaken. We tend to put great weight on our experiences, so when we have less experience, the premise weakens *much*. You're not sure what to do next. You no longer have confidence in your conclusions about what to say to your new manager or what might be expected of you with new responsibilities. You're not sure how to do things or what people look upon positively from newcomers. You are very uneasy about the change; it's that simple. That's why we don't like change; our premise generally becomes weaker, and we have less confidence that we know what to do.

As another example, let's say there's a change in a *process* you used in your job. You may have been able to follow the old process with your eyes closed, but you have no experience with this new one. You did undergo some training, but there's a lot to remember and apply. You're slower when you start implementing the new process; you have to refer to documentation frequently and aren't sure of the outcome or whether you're doing it right. You aren't familiar with the new process, so your premise that supports your conclusions about what choices to make and how to follow the process is weak. As a result, your confidence in implementing the process correctly is low. You don't like the change to the new process.

Our *ability to predict* significantly affects our attitude toward change. We have high confidence in the outcome of recurring events because we have a lot of experience and a strong premise. That's just another way of saying that we're better able to predict what will happen in these situations. If you obtained a certain result the last one hundred times you executed five steps of a process, then you naturally assume that the same result will occur if you execute those five steps again; that's just good old inductive reasoning.

Now we take away the experience, and give you a new system. You have no way to predict the outcome anymore—which is extremely unsettling.

Helping People Accept Change

How do you help people, or yourself, through change? Some managers simply advise employees to get over it. Unfortunately, that approach doesn't accomplish anything. If you want to help people accommodate change, you have to help them *increase their premise's strength*, thereby yielding confident conclusions. You're really helping instill confidence that people know what they're doing. One way to do that is to *give them time* to gain experience. However, that approach requires patience—and assumes that you *have* the time to do this. Most organizations and managers don't want to wait long enough for people to acclimate, so what else can you do? You can present additional facts (if available), but most of the time, the place to focus is on *observations and assumptions*.

Here's an example: your company has just rolled out a new computer application system that employees have to use. They have no experience with this new system, so their premises supporting what to do are weak. They were pros, but now they are novices concerned about making too many mistakes, especially when they used to be experts. One way to help these former-experts-turned-beginners would be to connect them with someone experienced with the new system, sometimes called a subject matter expert (SME). The SME uses his or her experience to tell the novice what to do (observations), thereby strengthening the novice's premise with these additional observations. As the novice performs these observations, he or she also starts to gain experiences. At the same time, the SME listens to the novice explain how to do something: "I think I should do it like this." The SME says, "That's right; that's exactly how you should do it." In this way, the novice's assumptions have been validated—and increased observations and validated assumptions yield a stronger premise. The premise becomes stronger, and novices' confidence in their conclusions goes up. They know what to do, how to do it, and, as a result, overcome their aversion to the change.

Getting Started with *Change*

Following are a few examples of when you might want to prepare for change by understanding what has changed and thinking about how to reinforce the premises to help people through change:

- *Process changes:* When you have to learn or teach entirely new procedures, or just a different order of steps, look for training opportunities to provide some basic experience and observations. Most important, ensure that a very well-trained individual can act as the SME resource, readily available for others who have to learn. SMEs will be able to offer their experiences and validate assumptions.

- *Organization-wide changes:* This is one of the most difficult changes for people. Not only might there be a new manager, and new responsibilities, but they also no longer have a clear picture of their job progression—and they can't predict what's going to change about their future. You can address their worry by being extremely clear regarding the change, new roles and responsibilities, and whether—or how—it affects people's jobs. Too often, organizational changes come first—*then* everyone scrambles to figure out what the communication messages should be. Plan ahead so that you can give people the information (observations) they need to be content with—or at least, to figure out—their futures.

- *Changes for customers:* Think about the change your customers will experience when you introduce a new product or service or eliminate an existing one. Ask *so what* about this modification to uncover how your customers are going to react. What's your reaction when a product *you* use changes or is not available, and you have to use something else? You make a few errors, things take longer, or the outcome isn't as good. You'll think how the old product was just great, and you have no experience with the new one. Although the change might be worth the effort to learn, it's still unpleasant. How are you going to communicate the change to your customers—and help them get over it?

Here are two general ways to help yourself and others adjust to change:

- *Realize that change is good.* It means you'll be learning new experiences to add to your premises. Your knowledge increases, and you become smarter, able to use your intelligence in a better way. That's a *good thing*, so ask yourself, How am I going to leverage this new opportunity? For instance, you're asked to move into a new position to help out another group. It's in an area that you're not that familiar with. Although the change will be tough, you'll learn a completely new set of skills that you'll be able to leverage your whole career. The change is good!

- *Acknowledge change.* If you change something, acknowledge you have just clobbered others' premises. Understand they will be uneasy about what to do next. Acknowledge that you know they have little experience with the new system or process, so now they may not have as much confidence in what to do. That's okay.

The Takeaway

Change generally means less experience, and that translates into a weaker premise. It diminishes your confidence in what to do. You can't predict. Strengthen the premise with additional observations and validated assumptions to increase confidence in the conclusion, and support the transition.

Exercises for Change

1. Try brushing your teeth with your other hand. What has changed, and how do you feel about it?

2. Watch someone who is learning how to operate a new piece of equipment or use a new computer application. You'll see their frustration. Ask them why they are frustrated.

(continued)

(continued)

3. Have a discussion with a peer about something that changed, what you learned, and what experiences of yours were no longer applicable.

4. Ask someone if he or she likes change. If the person says yes, ask what it is about change he or she likes. You'll probably get an explanation that includes "something new." These folks focus on the positive aspect of change—the learning. If the answer is no, ask what it is about change the person *doesn't* like. You'll probably get an explanation involving something he or she knew becoming obsolete. These folks focus on what they knew well and now can't use. What will *you* focus on the next time there is change?

26 Influencing and Persuading

Although you may be happy once you've formed your conclusions, you're not done yet—because you're not forming conclusions in a vacuum. Your boss may have to *approve* them, your reports need to *understand* them, and your peers are on the team helping you *implement* them. Not everyone will agree with your conclusion—and if that's the case, you may have to influence and persuade those who disagree.

The difference between influence and persuasion is whose conclusion is debated and to what degree things change. *Influence* is changing *others' conclusions*. It's *their* issue to resolve; you're communicating some of your premise items, such as your observations, to modify their premise and subsequent conclusions indirectly. *Persuasion* is directly *causing someone to adopt or concur with* your *conclusion*, which may at times be very different from his or her initial thinking.

Here's an example of a common headscratcher middle managers face: how can they influence senior management more? If you were one such middle manager, you'd first want to get clear on what *influence* means in this situation. Usually, it's to get senior managers to change something per your suggestion. You have influenced them if some of your ideas are incorporated in their ultimate conclusion.

Persuasion typically comes about when people use the word *get:* "How do I *get* them to agree with the way I want to do it?" or "How do I *get* them to do this task?" or "How do I *get* them to buy my product?" You have successfully persuaded someone if he or she agrees with you, adopts your conclusion, and does what you ask.

Influencing is generally more subtle than persuasion. Let's say you want to influence a coworker. You should expose him or her to new observations, experiences, and facts—not to change your coworker's mind directly, but as additional information you think he or she will find useful when forming *his or her* conclusion. If some of your components are then considered in his or her premise, you've done your job. His or her conclusion changes, because it must be consistent with the new premise components you introduced. You influenced your coworker's conclusion. For instance, let's say you're in sales, and you notice that Cheryl, a new sales associate, was preparing a pitch to an important customer about your new product. Her presentation started by introducing the exciting details of the new product. Having a lot of experience, you might wander over and say, "Hi, Cheryl. I used to be on that account. When I wanted to introduce a new product to them, what always worked for me was a conversation about the existing product first. This got them to talk about how much they liked it and got them in a great mood. Then I'd say, 'If you liked that, look what else I have to show you.' It worked every time." Cheryl listens to you explain your experience, which was an observation for her. You referenced that you used to be on that account (another observation for her), which gives credibility to your comments. With these observations, Cheryl modifies her presentation to lead with a short discussion of the benefits the customer is reaping from the current products. You've influenced her.

Persuasion is a *more direct method* of comparing premises, looking at the weighting behind premise elements, and moving someone from his or her conclusion to yours or another one. It is about attempting to sway a person's mind, changing a solution by convincing someone there's a better one out there. For example, your coworker says, "I think we need to test this with 10 of our customers," and you say, "I think we need to test this with at least 50." You present your premise components, one of which might be your experience in past tests with fewer versus more customers. After a brief discussion, your peer agrees that your experiences and observations are stronger than his or hers, and you have persuaded your peer to adopt your conclusion.

Whether it's influence or persuasion, the focus is to alter someone's conclusions—and the technique for both is very similar.

Using the Premise to Influence

We know that people use premises to form conclusions, so if you want to influence their conclusions, they need premise components to support the conclusion you want them to have. For example, let's say you want management to acknowledge employee accomplishments more. You might leave management an article about employees being much more engaged when management acknowledges their accomplishments. This observation strengthens the executive's premise for the headscratcher about how to motivate employees. Alternatively, perhaps you can have a casual conversation with the executive about employee morale and provide several examples of how acknowledging accomplishments makes a difference. Add applicable facts, observations, and experiences to the premise of the person making the conclusion. If these components are credible and consistent with his or her other premise items, they will influence him or her. If the new evidence is credible but not consistent with his or her premise components, he or she will at least pause to understand why.

In both cases, you influenced.

Using the Premise to Persuade

We're a little more active when persuading. If you want to change people's minds (their conclusions), you first need to understand the premises used to form their conclusions. If they feel firm about their conclusion, it's because they have (or think they have) a strong premise supporting it. There's only one way to change someone's mind: to weaken the premise that established the conclusion. This will cause doubt that the conclusion is a good one. Nobody wants to go down the road he or she thinks will lead to nowhere, so if you weaken one's premise, he or she will be open to another.
If you can show *your* premise is strong, he or she will have confidence in your conclusion—and will change his or her mind.

To weaken a premise, you must show how some facts are untrue, identify experiences contrary to what forms the premise, mention observations that question existing and weighted observations, and discover ways to invalidate assumptions.

Let's say you are in marketing, and you concluded to raise the price of one of your products. You inform the sales vice president (VP), who reacts by saying, "We'll be the highest priced product out there and won't be competitive, and customers won't buy it (assumption). Don't do it (conclusion)." Now is the time to start a premise conversation.

You ask, "Why do you think that because we're the highest priced, customers won't buy our product?" (That's an assumption the sales VP was making.)

The sales VP says, "At my past company, when we raised prices, we lost many of our customers" (experience).

You say, "Of course we'll probably lose a few, but our customer surveys indicate that they buy our product because of its unique functionality, and although price is a factor, it's way down the list of importance" (counterobservation). "Also, you sold a commodity product that was extremely price sensitive, whereas our product is unique, yes?" (counterobservation).

The sales VP says, "That's a good point."

You continue, "We are the leader, with a 60 percent market share (fact), and our value proposition isn't low price, but functionality (observation). We are the market leader because we solve the customers' needs better than anyone (assumption), and that's where our value is (observation). As a result, we can, and might even be expected, to be a little higher priced (assumption). Do you agree?" (You ask for agreement with your conclusion about raising the price.)

The sales VP says, "I do." In this conversation you were able to weaken the sales VP's premise by presenting credible observations that countered his assumption and experience. At the same time, you reinforced your assumptions with credible observations, facts, and experiences that the sales VP agreed with. You persuaded him. Nice job.

Maybe You Need to Be Persuaded?

Weakening the premise of another while strengthening yours will result in him or her losing confidence in their idea while gaining confidence in yours; you are persuading them and they will agree with your conclusion. Now consider reversing the process. Critical thinking isn't about winning debates or highlighting *your* ideas alone; it's about all ideas. It's not about your solution; it's about finding *the best* solution. In fact, it might be that *your* assumptions are invalid. As a problem solver, your job *isn't* to be the one who comes up with the idea about how to solve a problem; your job *is* to ensure that the problem is solved. If a solution you read in a book will work, even though it's not your idea, wouldn't you use it?

Don't be attached to your ideas to the detriment of considering others. Start conversations by considering multiple conclusions. The task is to figure out which one is most applicable and will do the best job. Know that if your premise is proven to be weak, you too will be happy to change your mind. After all, you should be open to what you're asking someone else to consider. Also, you'll think, "Thank goodness we had this conversation, because my way would not have achieved the results I anticipated."

Getting Started with *Influencing* and *Persuading*

Whatever you call it—influencing, persuading, buying in, convincing, or simply changing people's minds—the strategy is to evaluate the premise that supports the conclusions that we reach. Only then can you understand the basis of a conclusion and work to change it.

The following are some instances in which you can do so:

- *When your conclusion about how to accomplish something differs from someone else's:* Is the other person using inconsistent or dubious premise components? Can you provide any new observations or experiences that will be contrary to the ones currently used? Can you invalidate an assumption by showing in what circumstances that assumption would not be true? For example, you and your work associate just landed at San Francisco International Airport.

Your associate says, "Let's take a taxi from the airport to the city (conclusion)."

You say, "Bay Area Rapid Transit (BART)—the train—is easy, and it's a lot cheaper and faster (assumption). Let's take the train (conclusion)."

Your associate says, "They are on strike." Bam! He just invalidated your assumption about BART being easy and faster.

Your conclusion is no longer supported, and you say, "Taxi it is!" (Note: This actually happened to me!)

- *When you have an idea you want your boss to endorse:* There's nothing worse than when your boss asks you, "How did you arrive at that idea?" and you respond, "I just think it's a good idea." When you offer your solutions, be prepared to cite the assumptions you've made, and present the facts, observations, and experiences you used to arrive at those assumptions. Then show how you validated them. For example:

"Boss, I think we should extend our product warranty from 12 months to 18 months," you say.

"How did you reach that conclusion?" your boss asks.

"Well, in analyzing the data of thousands of purchases, only a handful of our products failed between the twelfth and eighteenth month (observation). So, one assumption I'm making is that very few customers have a problem with our products in that time frame; therefore, the cost to us is negligible. I'm also assuming that our customers will value our quality higher if we have an extended warranty. I validated the second assumption by way of a customer survey about how customers evaluate products. One factor high on the list was quality. When asked how they evaluated that, one of the top responses was how long the warranty is. Here's the data."

Your boss says, "Nice job; you've persuaded me."

- *When you're part of a conversation, and you're listening to others debate their points:* At this time, ask a few questions, such as what assumptions are being made and why. You might interject, "Have you seen this report?" (observation). That triggers a conversation, and from that, the merit of one premise might overshadow the merit of another, and agreement will follow—and then you'll have influenced.

- *When you're presenting (defending or suggesting a conclusion or asking for approval):* You can approach this in one of two ways: (1) start with the conclusion and then dive into the assumptions you made and why, or (2) start with facts, observations, and experiences and then show how these led to your assumptions, how you validated those assumptions, and therefore, why your conclusion is what it is.

You'll notice that I didn't discuss beliefs in this chapter. Although beliefs influence your premise, they're a tough place to start a conversation. Either people will agree with your belief or disagree; there is little in between. If they strongly disagree with it, your premise will be diluted, and they won't view your conclusion as a good one. If they agree with it, they still might discount it—because they might feel beliefs are personal and not for business, and therefore do not add to your premise's strength. However, if you know your boss is always seeking to do the right thing, then you might slip into a conversation with him or her, "Oh, by the way, this is also the right thing to do!" That's a home run, and you'll easily close the deal if the rest of the premise holds up.

The Takeaway

The purpose of influence and persuasion is to get others to change their conclusions. You do this by weakening the premise they've used to come to the original conclusion and strengthening a premise that supports another—thereby resulting in less confidence in the original conclusion and more confidence in the new conclusion. They change their minds. Be open to the possibility that if your premise weakens, you'll be the one who will be persuaded.

When you turn to the next chapter, you'll be entering a world of conclusions that go beyond those that you can form with the critical thinking methods we have so far presented. We call this *innovation*.

Exercises for Influence and Persuasion

1. How might parents influence their children to say please and thank you more?

2. If your newspaper delivery person delivered your newspaper by throwing it into your flower bed instead of your driveway, how would you persuade him not to do that? (Hint: He needs to conclude to deliver the paper on the driveway.)

3. When it comes time for salary reviews, how could you influence your boss for a raise?

4. Your project is running behind schedule. Some of your team members are working really hard but others are not. How can you persuade everyone to pull his or her weight? (Hint: Your conclusion is to work hard; theirs currently is not.)

5. It's budget time. How could you influence senior management to provide your department with a bigger budget for next year?

6. A new process has been introduced, but people are still using the old process. How would you persuade them to use the new process?

Section IV
Conclusions
and Innovation

Ralph Waldo Emerson is credited with uttering, "Build a better mouse-trap, and the world will beat a path to your door." The process of using inductive reasoning that starts with a premise to form our conclusion usually produces sound, executable, and reliable solutions—better mousetraps.

But what happens if a better mousetrap is not enough? What if you want to produce a true breakthrough, a paradigm-changing solution? Let's say revenue is flat, and the only solutions seem to be more marketing dollars, more salespeople, or an incremental product line revision. Someone asserts during a meeting, "Come on folks; we need to think *outside the box!*" Everyone starts to scramble for outside-the-box solutions. The trouble is that to think outside the box, you first have to know what the box is.

We define *innovation* and *creativity* as providing a new or modified conclusion that obtains a positive result. Innovation might be a customized process, fresh product, different marketing approach, or different way of handling a customer call.

What's the difference between regular conclusions and innovative conclusions? Well, there's no checklist to help differentiate. If a solution works, the problem is solved. Of course, there are ways to solve a problem that result in different outcomes. For example, maybe your headscratcher is to increase sales by 5 percent. There may be several solutions, but only one might enable sales to grow by 20 percent or accomplish the growth in half the time. These more powerful solutions are considered more innovative than the mere 5 percent increase because the results are better. Innovation doesn't have to be a *new* invention; it just has to produce *distinctive solutions*.

There are three critical thinking tools we use to generate results significantly beyond what simple conclusions can yield:

- Thinking outside the box
- Abductive thinking
- Impossible thinking

I'll detail these techniques in the next three chapters. You can use them in a variety of situations, ranging from "I have no idea what to do" to "Is there something even better than this?" to "We need a breakthrough idea." You won't use these techniques all the time, nor should you need to. The regular critical thinking process we use to reach conclusions via a premise should be sufficient—*most of the time*. That's where you should always start, because these other techniques rely on that process anyway.

Figure IV.1 illustrates the inductive or deductive premise-to-conclusions process we've already covered and how the new techniques enhance that process:

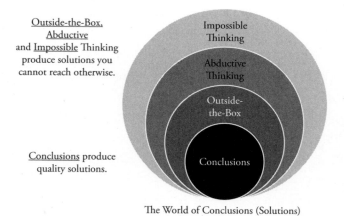

The World of Conclusions (Solutions)

Figure IV.1 The World of Conclusions (Solutions)

This figure shows four ways to think critically to arrive at solutions. The first and primary method is our basic, highly productive deduction and induction: facts, observations, experiences, beliefs, and assumptions comprise your premise, which results in a conclusion. As we know, this tactic yields quality solutions. Beyond our primary method of solving problems is outside-the-box thinking; then beyond that you have abductive thinking— and even beyond that, something our company calls impossible thinking. We're still in the world of conclusions, which these new tools enhance.

Innovation isn't reserved for the select few who come up with brilliant new products and ideas. Yes, those are surely innovative, and we classify most of those ideas as inventions. Everyone, however, can be innovative, especially when using critical thinking as a foundation. So let's begin the first chapter of this section with the not-so-clear phrase "think outside the box."

27 Outside-the-Box Thinking

"**W**e need to think outside the box!" someone passionately shouts during a meeting. The statement conveys the sense that the current thinking isn't yielding satisfactory solutions. Either they're not unique enough, or they won't produce the desired results.

When I hear this statement, I always ask, "What's outside the box?" The responses I get typically involve "away from the norm," "new and improved," "innovative," "radical," "no constraints," and "no preconceived notions." I nod and ask, "But what *is* the norm? What's the normal way we reach solutions?"

I'm happy to say that someone in our workshops usually remembers the prior hours' teachings and says, "Inductive reasoning, a premise yields conclusions. Facts, observations, experiences, beliefs, and assumptions."

I rejoice, "*Yes!*"

Your box is bound by your facts, observations, experiences, beliefs, and assumptions, so if you want to think outside of it, you have to think outside those boundaries. You'll still be using inductive reasoning, but with new or modified premise elements. You do this, as shown Figure 27.1, by pushing those boundaries.

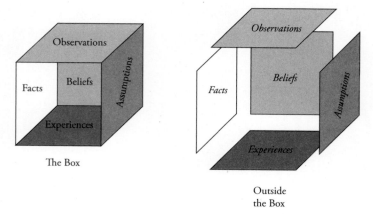

Figure 27.1 The Box

Try the puzzle shown in Figure 27.2. (You may wish to copy this page so that you don't give away the solution to someone who may read this book after you.) Place your pen or pencil on one of the dots, and without lifting your pen or pencil off the paper, without folding, mutilating, or destroying the paper, draw four straight lines connecting all the dots. Do this in the next 30 seconds. (Hint: Think outside the box.) The answer is at www.headscratchers.com/ThinkingOutsideTheBox.html.

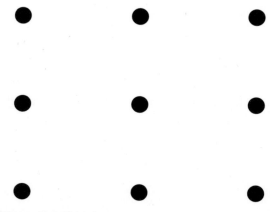

Figure 27.2 The 9-Dot Puzzle

When we conduct this exercise in our workshops, only a few people out of 20 or 25 are able to solve it. Some people think they solved it, only to realize they lifted their pens off the paper. The reality is that we like boundaries, and we like to stay inside our box—because boundaries are familiar. We have experiences with them and form strong premises with them that result in high-confidence conclusions. Going outside the boundaries feels unnatural to us. However, to solve the dot puzzle—and to *innovate*—you have to go beyond those boundaries and draw outside the box.

Ask *What If* and *What Other*

Now back to the real world. You go beyond the boundaries of your box by pushing on them with questions such as *"What if?"* What if I'm making an untrue or invalid assumption? What if I had your assumptions? What if *both* our assumptions are invalid? What if I'd never had that experience before? What if I did not read that memo? How would that affect my thinking? When thinking outside the box, you challenge the very premise that defines your box.

There was an accomplished financial investment analyst in a workshop I was conducting a few years ago. This was about a year after the financial collapse, now known as the deepest recession since the Great Depression. I invest in a few stocks, so I was eager to hear his view on what was happening. He had all kinds of data and charts, and his analysis was very thorough—comparing the recent stock market collapse to several prior collapses, steep drops, and recoveries over the past 80 years, including the Great Depression. He had comparisons that predicted when to sell, when to hold, and when to start buying, among other things. Like many other analysts at the time, he was determined to compare the 2008 crash to prior crashes, assuming that he could do so and make predictions for the future. His investment strategy for his clients followed that model. Of course, I was only a novice in stock investing, so who was I to question his thinking? However, I did ask one question: "What if your assumption about the current socioeconomic environment being comparable to the past is incorrect? What if this is the first of a *new kind* of financial collapse? What then?" Silence. Continued silence, followed by what looked like deep, deep thought. That one question pushed the financial analyst clear outside his box. As a result, he eventually came up with some new ideas with respect to managing his clients' portfolios. Of course, I didn't have the answer to the question *I* asked; I just asked the question as a thinking coach to provoke an outside-the-box view of the situation.

Follow the question "*What if* the assumptions are incorrect?" with "*What other* assumptions can I make?" and "How do those other assumptions change my thinking?" Follow "*What if* I've never had that experience?" with "*What other* experiences have I had that might change my thinking?" Follow "*What if* that memo I read is not accurate?" with "*What other* sources of information might provide me with new ideas?"

Getting Started with *Thinking Outside the Box*

Here are a few examples of when thinking outside the box is appropriate:

- *When someone says, "We need to think outside the box":* Clarify what the current box is, and then ask questions, such as "What if our assumptions are not correct?" or "What if we'd never had that experience?"

- *When solutions aren't forthcoming from the premise:* When the premise and its components are yielding more of the same—what you are doing or have tried already—that's the time to have an innovation discussion, starting with thinking outside the box.

- *When current solutions are fine, but you want to explore for a more significant result:* Use outside-the-box thinking to achieve a superb level of quality or increase revenue beyond expectations.

- *When there's a significant change:* When your competition introduces a significant threat (perhaps a major price reduction or new product), outside-the-box solutions might be warranted. Perhaps you're fortunate to encounter a huge opportunity and wish to take advantage; or you recently signed a hefty contract, and you'll need to hire a large number of people in a short period. The usual recruiting methods aren't going to fulfill that need in the allotted time. You need another solution.

- *When there is a crisis:* If a crisis occurs and you don't have a contingency plan already laid out, you'll probably need some outside-the-box ideas.

The Takeaway

To think outside the box, you have to acknowledge that the box is bound by your premise. You therefore have to push the box's sides and premise components to think outside of that. Use *what if* and *what other* to push on those boundaries and discover new ideas.

Exercises for Outside-the-Box Thinking

1. Think of a red brick. Take 30 seconds to write down everything you can do with a brick. Then review all unusual uses. What assumptions can you make about those uses?

2. When we are working on a project, we often assume that quality will suffer if we do it faster. What if that assumption were not true? What if your goal were to improve speed and quality at the same time? How would that change your thinking?

3. Let's say you were a vegetarian based on the belief that to raise animals solely for consumption is bad. But what if plants could think? How would that affect your thinking?

4. Most people look forward to retiring one day. What are your assumptions about your financial position and health at retirement age? What if these assumptions are incorrect?

28 Abductive Thinking

Warning: This chapter may shake up your world a little bit. You may never look at things the same way again.

An Educated Guess

Have you ever heard of abduction? (It has nothing to do with aliens.) It's an incredibly important kind of thinking but one that school generally doesn't teach. *Abductive thinking* is a guess. Guessing in critical thinking—how bizarre is that? But when your premise doesn't yield satisfactory solutions, inside or outside of the box, it might be time to look at abductive thinking.

You form *abductive conclusions* by using knowledge but *not experience*. It's an educated guess based on what you know. Therefore, abduction requires a deep, extensive knowledge base. Abduction supports Sir Francis Bacon's view that "Knowledge is power." Knowledge gives you choices. Where do you get most of your knowledge? From your experience. The more experience you have, the more knowledge you have.

As you can see, there's somewhat of a paradox to abductive thinking. You need an extensive base of knowledge to abduct (guess). More experience gives you more knowledge, but the more experience you have, the stronger your *inductive* reasoning—making it less likely that you'll guess, because you know already. For example, if I take 10,000 marbles out of a bucket, and all 10,000 are red, what will be the color of the next marble I take out of the bucket? Your 10,000 experiences make your premise very strong, so you would say "red" and be willing to wager on it. Of course, it could be blue; but there's a very low probability of that. The point is that you're not going to guess, because your premise is so strong that you think you *know* and that there is no value to guessing.

Figure 28.1 is an amazing, thought-altering illustration of a premise so strong that you'll completely lose the ability to consider any other possible answer. Take a look at the checkerboard illustration, and describe the shading for the squares labeled A and B. Dark gray and light gray, right? What if I told you they were identical shades of gray—no, not the letters, the actual checkerboard squares labeled A and B? Well, they are. Make a copy of this page, and cut out a piece from square A. Now move that piece to square B. Now move it back. Do the same thing with piece B. Cut it out, move it to A, and then move it back. Are you freaking out yet? Yes, they are both the same shade, and they are both dark gray. How is this possible?

There are three things going on here:

1. A long time ago, you were born. Soon after you were born, you opened your eyes and you saw shadows. Where there are light and objects, there are shadows. There are shadows all around you, and you've seen them trillions and trillions of times. Based on your experience with shadows, you know things in shadows are really lighter than they appear, so your brain assumes B is lighter.

2. You also saw perspective when you opened your eyes; that is, things farther away were darker than closer things. You've seen that trillions of times, too, so you assume square A, being farther away, is darker than B.

3. Last, you're a pattern recognition machine, and you've seen this checkerboard pattern many times. We've seen in Chapter 1 how our mind assumes, distorts, and discards things so that what we experience fits a pattern.

Therefore, you have an unbelievable amount of experience with shadows, perspective, and patterns. Your inductive reasoning is so incredibly strong here that your brain says, "Eyes, you must be having a really bad day,

Figure 28.1 Strong Inductive Reasoning at Work

because you are sending me information that makes no sense, so I will change it." Your brain alters what the eyes see and makes it wrong. Squares A and B are the same shade of gray, yet because of an overwhelmingly strong premise, your brain changes the shades to match its conclusion and completely ignores evidence to the contrary. There is no consideration that another possibility could exist.

Old Dog Thinking

Your inductive reasoning in the preceding example is so incredibly strong that there is no opportunity or capability to guess another outcome. You've heard the expression "You can't teach an old dog new tricks." Usually this refers to someone who has been in the same job for a long time, when his or her response to having to learn something new is "Hey, I've been doing this for 30 years. I know how to get this done." However, in the checkerboard example, it's not that you don't want to see it; you *cannot* see it. We call that *old dog thinking*—where your experience is so strong that you can't see any other solutions. You lose the ability to abduct because there's no need to guess, because you know.

The real world isn't quite like the checkerboard example. You have experiences from your job but not trillions of them. The difference is that although your very strong premise prevents you from seeing another solution, your reaction when someone points out something new to you is often, "Ah, of course, why didn't *I* think of that?" The truth is, you would have never thought of it. Your inductive reasoning is too strong.

Your experience is valuable, so don't discard it. Just know that it means you are less likely to guess at another solution because there's no need to guess; you know.

Knowledge with No Experience

Abductive thinking requires knowledge but only works when there isn't much experience. How do you do that? There are two ways:

- If you're trying to solve a problem but have no experience with it, it's easy to abduct. You have to gain knowledge, so you read, ask questions, and research—all of which allow you to learn despite your lack of experience. At some point, you've gained enough knowledge to say, "I think I know what's going on here, and based on what I've read, the solution is this." For example, the Internet gives people access to a tremendous amount of information in the medical field. If you have a pain somewhere in your body, you can use the Internet to get all kinds of information about pains and other symptoms. (Note: Not everything you read on medical websites is credible.) You can accumulate an incredible amount of medical knowledge just by reading. However, you have no experience, so you guess, or self-diagnose, your problem—which can lead to some very bad conclusions and a great deal of anxiety. However, your guess might be spot-on and different from what someone with experience might conclude.

- If you have experience in the subject matter, then you'll need to team up with someone knowledgeable who doesn't have very much experience. Your experience will make your inductive reasoning strong, but the person you teamed with will have to come to conclusions based on knowledge and guesses. You'll be surprised how many times you utter, "That's a great idea. I would not have thought of that."

Old Dog Thinking Cures

What's the cure for old dog thinking? There are a few things you can do:

- *You can't ask yourself in what ways are you an old dog, because you can't see it. However, you can ask yourself, "Where do I run the risk of being an old dog?"* The following was a wake-up call for me. I was eating in a restaurant with my family, and I observed another family with two middle school–aged children enter and sit at a table near us. The two children were using their phones, and after a few minutes it became obvious to me they were texting each other, despite sitting across the table from each other. I said to my daughter, "Look at that, they can't even have a conversation with each other; they have to text." My daughter turned to me and said, "Dad, they're having a private conversation." Hmm— they were talking about something they didn't want their parents to hear. Rudeness aside, I thought that was amazing; I'd never thought of using phones that way. Because of that evening, I thought about my very technical background and asked myself: Where do I run the risk of being an old dog with respect to technology? For me, it is being unable to recognize a new world of communication, be it private, public, or even with our HeadScratchers training. Using texting, Facebook, and Twitter in training? I'm not there yet, but I'm sure there's a use for them. When the time comes, I'll need to team up with a Generation X, Y, or Z person for help, because I won't see it.

- *You can team up with a knowledgeable person who has less experience than you.* He or she will ask you the seemingly stupid question you'll never ask because you know better. He or she will try something because he or she doesn't know it won't work—and maybe it'll actually work this time. Watch kids build something. They don't have much experience in materials, engineering, or physics, or years and years of experiencing the mistakes you have.

For several years, I was a coach with the Destination Imagination organization (www.idodi.org) for a team of seven kids of elementary and middle school age. The teams receive huge challenges—some technical, some theatrical, and some a mixture—and compete to see whom the judges deem best. One year, the team members chose a difficult technical challenge, and came up with a few solution designs. I said to myself, "Oh, that's just never going to work." However, as a coach in this organization, you aren't allowed to help the team (which is good practice for being a thinking coach). I couldn't tell the team it was a bad idea; they'd have to figure that out it for themselves. They discovered a few things that didn't work, and I of course thought, "I knew that wouldn't work." Then they tried one idea I was *certain* would fail, and it worked. I was amazed. Based on my experience with materials, building, weights, and kids' talents (or lack thereof), I was positive their design couldn't be successful; I would have never tried it. The lesson here is, ask someone with less experience than you to help, watch, make suggestions, and ask stupid questions. One of those questions might not be stupid and might generate an idea or solution you never would have imagined.

Some of my clients have a great process for fighting old dog thinking. When they are working on a technical problem to solve, they put their very experienced people in a room with some junior folks. For the first 30 minutes or so, only the junior people can ask questions. You have to make it very safe for them to ask loads of stupid questions. Every so often, they'll ask a question that will prompt one of the senior folks to follow with, "Why did you ask that question?" When the junior person explains, the response from the senior people is sometimes, "Wow, that's a great idea. I would have never thought of that," and that's precisely the point.

- *Watch out for expressions such as "That's a no-brainer" or "It's obvious."* Something is *obvious* when there is strong inductive thinking, and you have a strong premise. It's a no-brainer if you now have to do something you've done before a hundred times with the same result. You've done it so much; why think of anything else? Although this works often, you've halted abductive thinking at the expense of new ideas.

Getting Started with *Abductive Thinking*

Here are a few times to employ abductive thinking techniques:

- *When you have a room filled with experienced senior people:* You'll have great experiences and many solutions that leverage that experience; but it's all old dog thinking. It's time to ask the question "Where do we run the risk of being an old dog?" (Take care asking this question because some may take offense because of the traditional definition of *old dog*. Perhaps read them this chapter first.) Bring some junior people into the room, and make it safe for them to ask stupid questions—because some of the questions might be terrific.

- *When you hear, "It's obvious":* Understand the experience that made this conclusion so *obvious*. Ask what else is possible if the obvious solution were not available.

- *When you have no experience at all:* You have no choice but to gain knowledge and guess a solution. Perhaps your kids ask you to help them plant a vegetable garden, but you grew up downtown in a large city neighborhood, and the closest to a garden you've ever been was a flower shop. Do some reading, and then guess at solutions for the garden. You might also want to check with someone with experience. Although some of your guesses might be brilliant, some will be stupid and your kids might not be as patient as your coworkers.

- *When existing solutions no longer work:* It's then time to discard experience and start over from your knowledge outside of that experience. Perhaps you're in sales, and you've spent 20 years successfully closing deals face to face, with in-store customers. People are using the Internet to buy differently now. You no longer get to shake their hands, so—what next?

The Takeaway

Your experience is a tremendous asset. It means your inductive reasoning and premise are very strong, and you have a high-confidence conclusion. Inductive reasoning works most of the time, but there's a risk of old dog thinking—when your inductive reasoning is so strong that you lose the ability to guess or see another idea. Combat this by identifying where you run the risk of being an old dog and teaming with less experienced people.

Exercises for Abductive Thinking

1. List three frequent activities where you run the risk of being an old dog—where you have so much experience that you're unlikely to recognize other opportunities. These can be professional processes or parts of your personal life.

2. You may have seen the commercial containing the expression "Ah, I could have had a V8," as the actor suddenly discovers he could have had V8 to drink instead of the usual refreshment choices. This is an example of the reaction when someone doesn't see an idea and then all of a sudden sees it. Think of a time when you had that aha moment, that "Duh, I can't believe I didn't think of that" moment. That's what an abductive moment feels like.

3. Watch some kids build something, and listen carefully to their conversation about how they think things work. Ask them a few questions, such as, "Why do you think that will work?" You'll be amazed.

29 Impossible Thinking

Thinking about How to Accomplish the Impossible

We've looked at thinking outside the box and abductive thinking. For a tool to really take your mind beyond boundaries, look no further than *impossible thinking*. You take your headscratcher and expand it so that it's *impossible* to solve. Then you ask the question: If you *had to* solve this problem—if it were necessary to solve or if you would die if you didn't solve it—what would you do?

A few things happen when you have an impossible conversation. First, it's a ridiculous conversation, so you acknowledge that everything said or suggested—the whole conversation—is stupid. As a result, quiet folks with great ideas start to speak up, because nothing discussed can be incorrect. Even more exciting, the ridiculous ideas normally shot down are now acceptable. Because the whole conversation is impossible, every idea is a good one, no matter how impossible. Even more amazing, because it's an impossible conversation, your brain can't make the determination that a thought isn't important, so it no longer discards ideas.

This simple exercise will demonstrate impossible thinking. Remember the nine dots exercise in "Outside-the-Box Thinking," in which you had to connect the dots using four lines without lifting pen from paper? Now do it with one line. (*Try it before reading the next sentence.*) In our workshops, someone usually shouts within 5 to 10 seconds, "Use a thick marker!" Nobody makes that suggestion when it's possible to do so while thinking outside the box, but because this problem is impossible, someone makes the suggestion very quickly. Why is that? Impossible conversations have no constraints and no reality, so anything goes. You no longer throw away ideas because they're silly; instead, you vet those ideas.

Some of our clients are in the pharmaceutical industry. In our company's innovation workshops, I ask how long it takes from the moment a lab scientist says, "Gee, a cure for disease X" to when a drug hits the market. The response I usually get is 10, 12, or even 15 years. When I ask what it would take to accomplish that in an average of nine years, I get responses such as "A lot of red tape would have to be cut" or "Not going to happen." Then I ask if the whole process could take six months, and I nearly get thrown out of the room. That goal is unilaterally considered completely and utterly impossible. Then I frame the following scenario: suppose there's a virus called Q1X5, and it's highly contagious—so contagious that merely walking by a carrier would cause you to contract this killer. If you are infected with Q1X5, there's a 50 percent chance you will die within a year. As a result, a high percentage of Earth's population would die in less than three years. Clearly, this is a bad situation. Now enter a lab scientist who looks closely at his experiment and says, "Gee, look at this, a vaccine for Q1X5." I ask the class, "How long do you think it would take to get that drug into the marketplace?" The participants in the class shout answers— weeks, maybe a month or two. "What?" I inquire. "You thought nine years was tough, and you almost threw me out of the room when I asked for six months. What's changed here?" They respond that the necessity would make them able to eliminate lab testing and go straight to humans; they could go to the front of the Food and Drug Administration (FDA) line and skip clinical trials, and the FDA would lift the requirements for studying side effects. Of course, many of the solutions raised in this workshop were ridiculous and impractical, but trying to solve the impossible surfaced a number of initiatives that could be accomplished. Although they won't solve the impossible, the initiatives would make a huge difference in getting the time down to 9 years from 10 or 12.

Getting Started with *Impossible Thinking*

Here are a few places to consider using impossible thinking:

- *When you're running low on ideas to solve a headscratcher, when traditional or outside-the-box ideas are coming close but not providing adequate solutions:* Say you've got a plan that increases sales by 7 percent, but you need to get to 10 percent. The room is quiet, and no one is bringing new ideas forth. Challenge the group to grow sales by 50 percent, or everyone is fired. (You had no alternative but to do this.) You won't get to 50 percent, but the very act of setting an overwhelming goal will generate new ideas, and that extra 3 percent you seek will appear easy to achieve by comparison.

- *When everyone says it can't be done:* You're working on a project estimated to take 18 months. Someone asks if it can be done in 16, and everyone immediately says no way. Now is the time to ask for it to be done in six months. If you had to get it done in six months, or the competition would eat your lunch, and you'd be left in the dust with fewer people, no revenue, and no customers—what would you do?

- *When you want to have fun solving a difficult problem:* Impossible conversations are fun. Everything goes, and some ideas are so wacky they're laughable. Others are so ingenious you'll chuckle at why it took an impossible conversation to expose them.

- *When the possible isn't going to cut it:* When the problem is so deep that ordinary solutions won't work. Think about companies teetering near collapse because of tardy response to technology or market changes. They are, or were, in a nearly impossible situation. Regular, outside-the-box, and abductive thinking won't get them out of a seemingly impossible issue; they need impossible thinking to have a shot. If you're a brick-and-mortar retail shop selling goods available from dozens of online retailers, and your store traffic is plummeting, you need some impossible thinking. For example, what would you do if you had to get 10 times as much foot traffic into your store tomorrow as you did today, or you would go out of business?

The Takeaway

Ask about solving the impossible to uncover ideas that contribute to solving the possible.

Exercises for Impossible Thinking

1. What would you do if you had to sell 10 times the volume of product that you normally sell over the course of the next 30 days? Did you generate any ideas that could contribute to a more modest goal of a 10 percent increase in sales?

2. What if global warming was chronic and immediate, and we would all suffocate in five years unless the world dramatically decreased carbon emissions? What do you think we would do? How would you get to work? How would you get home? What would you eat?

3. If you had to cut your personal expenses by 75 percent, what would you do? Are there any ideas you can apply to reduce your expenses by 10 percent?

4. If your normal product development cycle took 18 months, what would you have to do to shorten it to 3 months? What can you implement now?

30 Summary of Conclusions

Creating Solutions

We started this section by discussing inductive reasoning, critical think-ing that leverages what we do thousands of times a day. We learned that it's all about the premise—the facts, observations, experiences, beliefs, and assumptions that we combine to come up with conclusions. We looked at ways to ensure a strong premise through credibility, consistency, and triangular thinking. We learned influencing and persuading is about having a strong premise and weakening others' premises, why change is hard, and how to address that difficulty. We moved on to innovative solutions with outside-the-box, abductive, and impossible thinking. These latter techniques produce solutions the ordinary premise-to-conclusion critical thinking process won't.

Getting Started

Problem solving and accomplishing things is the purpose of finding conclusions. Ask these questions when you're looking for a solution:

- What assumptions can I make? (Or, what assumptions am I making?)
- Why am I making those assumptions?
- Can I validate those assumptions?

- What conclusions can I reach based on those assumptions derived from facts, observations, and experiences?

- Are my premise components credible?

- Are my premise components consistent with each other and other things I know?

- Can I indirectly triangulate on a solution? (Or, do I get conflicting answers if I look at this situation from multiple perspectives?)

- Given my conclusion, how can I persuade others to endorse this solution?

- How can I defend my conclusion?

- How can I influence others with my premise components?

- If we move forward with this solution, how are we going to help people through the change?

- What if my assumptions are incorrect? What if I didn't have that experience? What outside-the-box ideas do these questions generate?

- How is my thinking an old dog risk? What actions can I take to combat being an old dog?

- What if we set a goal so high for my headscratcher that it becomes impossible? What new ideas are generated to help achieve the possible?

Sorry, You're Not Quite Done!

Creating solutions is the main goal in problem solving, but you're not finished. Just because you figured out what to do doesn't mean you'll do it. You have to decide to take action and do it. It may not be your decision, so before you can take action, someone else may need to decide. Therefore, we are now ready for decisions, the last—and easiest—step in critical thinking.

Section V
Decisions

Decisions can come very fast when you follow the critical thinking framework, because you've already done the heavy lifting in getting clear and concluding. You are clear on what the headscratcher is, and you have reached conclusions to solve it. Now it's a matter of acting—doing it or not doing it, deciding it's a go or no-go.

You might wonder why decisions have to be a separate step, if they're really just a call to go or no-go. Well, there are two reasons. First, although you might be the one responsible for solving a problem, you may not be the decision maker with respect to *approving action*. As a result, someone else has to do some thinking to approve it. Second, just because you figured out what to do doesn't mean it automatically starts to happen. You have to act (or decide not to act) and think differently than you did for clarity and conclusions to do so. As an example, take your to-do list. Although you *concluded* to do these tasks (that's why they're on your list), you haven't *decided* to do them—or they would be checked off your list.

We use just a few tools to help make decisions. First, we identify *who* the decision maker is. We often think we're the decision maker when we're actually the recommender. This doesn't make our job any easier; it just means we're not the individual responsible for signing off on the go or no-go. If your manager has to approve your action—even if it's something seemingly trivial—then he or she is the decision maker, not you. In addition to identifying who is the decision maker, you should know by *when* the decision needs to be made, as well as the *need* behind the decision (yes—decisions have needs, too). The central tool for decisions is the *criteria* used to decide. This is the decision maker's checklist of thresholds that must be met for him or her to say, "Go." Last, a key component of the criteria is the *risk* perspective of a particular decision. We use these tools to decide whether to say yes or no.

Now we'll put the decision process to work by way of example. If you have reached the conclusion "I want to read about decisions," then the decision you should now make is to turn the page to the next chapter.

31 Who, Need, and When

Whose Decision Is This, Anyway?

You've worked hard in getting clear on a headscratcher and concluding the best solution for it. Everyone on the team is ready to go, but there's one more potential issue: you may need someone else's approval to proceed. Although you likely have authority to make some decisions, not all of them are your call, perhaps because you need additional budget, resources, or capital expenses that are beyond your authority. Maybe you need approval to shift priorities enough to begin. If it's not your decision, you go to your manager for approval. He or she too makes many decisions, but unfortunately, his or her response is sometimes, "Oh, that's not my call. We'll have to ask my manager." Then sometimes, the *next* response is, "Oh, we need several people to approve this." Sometimes, it gets even worse in a large company. Then the response might be, "Gee, I'm not sure *who* needs to approve this."

In most cases, a single person is responsible for the decision. Others, such as peers or staff, may be consulted for opinions and concurrence, but at the end of the day, it's usually up to one person to decide whether something is a go or no-go. Some organizations have voting committees, and decisions need a majority—or occasionally even unanimous—affirmative vote to get approval. For example, a steering committee's purpose is to control a company's direction. It accomplishes this by saying yea or nay on projects and initiatives and by setting priorities. Committees usually have a chairperson—often the senior executive—who says yea or nay after listening to the committee's views. In any case, it's crucial to know who will make the decision: whether it's you, another individual, or a committee. You must appeal to decision makers, because they're the ones who weigh factors, including the criteria to make the call.

Need, Again!

Similar to *need* in clarity—why the headscratcher needs to be solved—the *need* in decisions identifies why someone has to make this decision. It also includes what that particular decision maker's need is for deciding. Many times it's because he or she is accountable for the results related to the headscratcher. If the problem isn't solved or the goal is not achieved, his or her personal performance is on the line. If the decision maker disassociates from a need—that is, if he or she doesn't think the decision affects him or her at all—then it's much harder to get a decision from that person. Your proposal just sits on a desk, waiting for it to reach the top of the stack—someday. If you want decisions made quickly, ensure that the decision maker is clear on how the decision will satisfy needs.

For example, you've concluded that you'll need to hire another person to produce the forecasted product quantity. After this conclusion, you make other conclusions, such as opening a hiring requisition. Who approves the decision to hire someone? Perhaps it's your manager. The human resources (HR) department usually plays a part as well, because a new hire adds head count to the overall employee base. Therefore, you need two approvals. You'll present the need for the business using the premise elements of your conclusion and persuade your manager, as well as HR, that the business need is there. Your manager is responsible for the department's results, so he or she has a personal stake and a need to ensure product availability. HR's need is to ensure that employees have an opportunity to grow and perhaps move across the company. They must also keep the head count within the overall company strategy. Knowing this, you may have to show how approving your requisition can help them satisfy *their* need as well.

When Does This Decision Need to Be Made?

Another key component to decision making is identifying by when the decision needs to be made. If you've concluded to watch a movie that starts at 8:30 PM at the local theater, then you need to go to the movie by that time or you're going to miss it. Figuring out when a decision is due is easy with time-dependent choices like this; if you don't make the decision by a certain point, then the headscratcher is automatically defaulting to no-go—no action taken, or no change in condition, because no decision was reached to affect anything.

Because time-dependent decisions have a clear timeline, always ask if the decision has a definitive stop—sometimes called a *drop-dead date*. After then, it's too late. The difficulty with time-independent decisions lies in establishing a deadline, because most initiatives take time to implement. If the time to implement a conclusion is four months, the decision to start implementation would have to be four months before you need it completed. There's wiggle room here, because the decision maker might assume (perhaps mistakenly) that a few days' delay—or even a week or more—won't affect the schedule.

The worst response you can give or get when someone asks, "When does this have to be decided?" is "As soon as possible (ASAP)." What does ASAP even mean? It's certainly not very clear; it could mean when I can get to it, when I have nothing better to do, today, tomorrow, or next week. ASAP is not a date and makes the real date unclear. Set a date for the decision.

One reason to identify and set a date is that it *generates a need*. If you commit to a date, and one of your beliefs is to do what you say you'll do, then you have artificially created a need—and now you have to decide. It's a purposeful setup, so remember, "Necessity is the mother of invention." Make sure you have a date by when the decision *needs* to be made.

Getting Started with *Who*, *Need*, and *When*

Here are some ideas about when and how to focus on the *who*, *need*, and *when* for a decision:

- *Identify the decision maker as soon as you reach a conclusion:* The person responsible for making a decision depends upon the conclusion you reach. If your headscratcher relates to a marketing program, *you* might be able to make the decision for an ad's copy; but your *manager* may have to decide where to place the ad, and your *director* may have to approve the budget. Before you invest too much time in the details of your conclusion, get an early read from the decision maker with respect to any considerations about your conclusion. This ties closely into the criteria you'll read about in the next chapter.

- *Ensure that there* is *a need:* Although you may have avoided the question of need during clarity, you can't dodge it now. You and your company have many things to do, and your decisions initiate actions that require resources, money, and time. The decision maker will use all three sparingly—so unless you can identify the need, you risk a negative decision or at the very least a wait or hold.

- *Identify a date when, if past, it's too late to decide:* Dates can drive need. If the decision date isn't definitive, then need doesn't exist now—even if there is a need. There's simply no immediate pressure to decide. A *later need* with no date is really a *no need*, so set a realistic, justified date by when you must make a decision to satisfy the need. If you cannot, then reconsider why you're suggesting this initiative in the first place.

The Takeaway

Identifying both the decision maker and a decision-making timeline that includes the need to make it will ensure that you and your group come to a timely decision.

Exercises for Who, When, and Need

1. Look at your to-do list. Are you the decision maker for each of the items on it? Are you sure? When does each item need to be completed, and why is it necessary to decide by that time?

2. Look ahead (ask *what's next*) at a decision you will make. Who is the decision maker? By when must that decision be made? What is the business need for the decision? What is personal need of the decision maker to make it?

3. Write down 10 decisions for which you are responsible at work and at home. Ask yourself: Do you need someone else to sign off on this? Do you need your significant other, a family member, or a friend to agree before you will proceed? If so, you are not the decision maker—or at least not the *sole* decision maker.

4. Let's say that you were to look for another position, either within your company or elsewhere. Write down six decisions to make and who the decision maker is. For example, one decision might actually be to *look* for another position, another might be to relocate to another state, and another might be for you to accept another job offer. Who helps decide in all of these steps?

32 Criteria

Without Criteria, Nothing Is Decided

Criteria are conditions that, if met, lead to a decision of yea—and if not met, the decision is nay or deferred to a later time. Suppose you concluded to buy a television because your existing one no longer works and needs to be replaced. Your family need is that everyone in your household likes to watch television—at least occasionally—so you consider this item essential to family entertainment. Your personal need is that your family will drive you crazy if you don't replace the television.

Let's say *you* are the decision maker in this scenario, and you've set a date to replace the television within three days from now. Off you go to the store. Do you buy just any television? Price probably comes into play, and perhaps financing. Other criteria might be size, picture quality, and perhaps number of plug-ins and other features, such as USB, HDMI, RGB, wireless, Internet readiness, and an internal alarm clock. You have your features checklist, and if you find a television meeting those criteria, then you'll buy it. If you walk into the store without criteria, you'll spend far longer evaluating televisions. You may not consciously make a list, but eventually, you *will* have criteria for purchasing. If you do a little critical thinking and understand the purchase criteria, you'll decide much more quickly.

Although it's not frequently written down anywhere, decision makers in business use the same process. Let's say you were asked to streamline a process to reduce manufacturing costs. After getting clear on the issues, you conclude to eliminate and combine some steps, shuffle some responsibilities, and implement a training program. The cost could be $20,000, with the payback projected to be about two years. You have a conversation with your manager and create a decision criteria checklist:

- Costs less than $25,000: yes/no
- Payback less than three years: yes/no
- Training program identified: yes/no
- Cost reduction greater than 20 percent: yes/no
- Night shift manager agrees with change: yes/no

You review your conclusions and the criteria, and you say, "Yes, Yes, Yes, Yes, Yes." Your manager says, "Go." Of course, if you had responded "No" to any of these criteria, your manager also would have said, "No," or "You'll need to meet these criteria before I can say yes." At that point, you would've had to go back and adjust your plan.

It's best to set the criteria for a decision as far ahead of the conversations for approval as possible. This way, you don't first learn about a criterion while you're seeking approval. You avoid going back to determine whether you meet the new criterion, then returning for approval and presenting your case again.

What happens if you *can't* have a criteria conversation? There are some situations where this is the case; say, for example, that your boss's boss's boss will decide. He travels often, and you're just never going to have that conversation. You then have to ask yourself: What criteria would you use if it were your decision? The closer you get to the decision maker's criteria, the less interaction you'll need with him, and the faster the decision will come.

Getting Started with *Criteria*

Here are some things to remember about using criteria:

- *Identify the decision maker as soon as you reach a conclusion:* Start by asking yourself what you think the criteria should be. If you have access to the decision maker, ask what criteria, if met, will get a yea.
- *Take the first stab at criteria:* Don't approach your manager with a blank page and ask him or her to list the criteria for a decision. He or she is likely to say, "When it makes business sense"—which doesn't help very much. Instead, start your criteria list, and ask your manager if it looks

right or if there are other criteria you should add. Doing so is more efficient and generates a more in-depth response.

- *List criteria that matter:* Although some features are nice to have, criteria should be those items when if met produce a go, and if not met produce a no-go. If you're buying a new phone, and it really doesn't matter if it's black or white, then don't put that down as a criterion. If the screen size matters, then make it a criterion.

The Takeaway

Decisions require a checklist, a list of criteria with which to decide. If the conditions are met, you act. Without conscious criteria, you make no decision—or a bad decision.

Exercises for Criteria

1. Go back to your to-do list. Those items remain there because you either don't have the need to do them or haven't figured out criteria for accomplishing them. What satisfied criteria will initiate action?

2. It's Friday afternoon, and you conclude to visit a close relative tomorrow. It's a three-hour drive. The 11:00 PM news calls for bad weather. What criteria would you use Saturday morning to decide whether to visit your relative?

3. A customer asked to return a new microwave oven she purchased because it no longer worked. Your warranty is 90 days, yet she purchased the oven 110 days ago. She explained she was out of the country for a month. You concluded she can bring in the microwave oven, and you'll replace it. She arrives with her microwave. What conditions (criteria) will you use to decide whether to replace the oven?

33 Risk

What's the Risk?

Because the *risk* criterion is always present, it deserves its own chapter. Risk is reflected in pro-versus-con or upside-versus-downside conversations. As you likely know, a con or downside is the negative result of a decision—something that prompts us to ask, "What's something bad or unexpected that could occur?" Everyone views risk differently. The probabilities of certain outcomes are the same, but people interpret and apply them uniquely. As a result, a decision might be yea for some and nay for others.

Let's say your net worth was $100,000. You're in Las Vegas for a vacation, and you decide to play at the roulette table. Would you place a bet of $10,000, with the risk of losing it all at once? Probably not: that's 10 percent of your entire assets. If you lost it, you would negatively impact your livelihood in a significant way. Would you place a $1 bet? Sure, because it's only one-thousandth of 1 percent of your assets. If you lost $1, it wouldn't affect you at all. You're next to another player whose net worth is $1 billion. For the billionaire, that same $10,000 bet would be one-thousandth of 1 percent of his assets, as $1 is to your $100,000. Although most billionaires are smart enough not to waste $10,000, there would be virtually no impact on them if they did. Although the statistical probability of losing $10,000 is the same for you as it is for the billionaire, the total risk of losing the $10,000 is very different between the two of you. The downside for both is losing $10,000, but the effective downside for the billionaire is much, much less than it is for you.

Here is another example. Let's say you're in the auto business and have to conduct a product recall because of a possible manufacturing defect. Your engineers, attorneys, and statisticians tell you the probability of catastrophic failure is very low—less than 1 in 100,000—and of annoyance failure (that is, annoying issues that are fairly easy to solve) is less than 1 in 1,000. It is possible for someone to get seriously hurt in a catastrophic failure. Do you take the risk of not initiating a voluntary recall? The numbers by themselves won't give you a go or no-go—and there are clear risk factors inherent in this situation. Can you handle the bad press, lawsuits, and even personal remorse if something bad happens? If your values include doing the right thing, then is it necessary to have the recall? We look at a number of factors collectively when evaluating risk. Although the factors are common among all of us, we each weigh them differently. Depending on the weight we give each, some people might consider them too risky, whereas others deem them not *that* risky.

Have you ever said this to someone: "What's the worst thing that can happen if you ask for that? " When you're concerned about requesting something—a raise, a new job, directions, permission, even someone to marry you—you risk being turned down. That's disappointing and embarrassing. In the case of asking for a raise, you might worry you're jeopardizing future opportunities. These are all downsides, and although perhaps unlikely, they all are possible. You're not afraid to *ask;* you're afraid of the downside, and you haven't figured out how you would recover or if you could reverse the damage. On the other hand, the upside to these conclusions is very significant. Although the downside could occur, you decide to take the chance.

11 Risk Factors

Critical thinking requires that we analyze risk beyond upsides and downsides. We look at factors about which we're concerned, afraid, and reluctant. To that end, HeadScratchers created a model of 11 factors to consider when evaluating risk—shown in Figure 33.1.

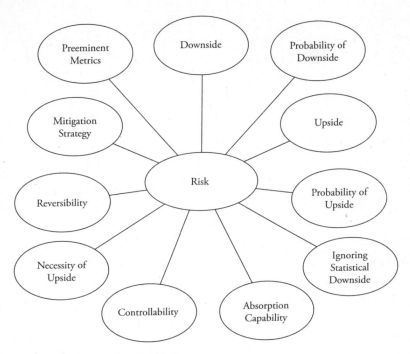

Figure 33.1 Evaluating Risk

1. *Downside:* This is a bad outcome that is a possibility based on a given decision. It defines the potential negative impact if the risk occurs. A professional downside could be losing a customer, having an employee quit, being sued for $10 million, or having your competition take the lead. On a personal level, a downside might be appearing foolish, losing $10,000, breaking a leg or arm, or death (the most extreme, of course).

2. *Probability of the downside:* For example, what's the *chance* you might die in a car accident or get hit by lightning? These statistics exist. However, other downsides—such as the chance of someone saying no if you proposed marriage or your boss firing you because you asked for a raise—are not calculable. You assign your own probability, which is actually a conclusion derived. If you conclude the downside will probably not occur, you'll assign a low probability to the risk. But if you conclude that it's likely to happen, you'll assign a high probability—and possibly avoid taking the action.

3. *Upside:* This is the benefit to the decision, the reason you're taking action in the first place. For example, a decision to open a new store in another location would increase presence and sales. The benefits of introducing a new product are to stay competitive, expand your market, and increase your sales.

4. *Probability of the upside:* This is the likelihood of achieving the upside. In most cases this is high, because you would conclude a different solution if you didn't think you could achieve this one.

A note about upsides and downsides: When you evaluate risk and downsides, you contemplate the upside, too. If the upside is a small benefit, and the downside is dreadful (although unlikely), you probably won't chance it. For instance, if the upside of waiting on a manufacturing maintenance cycle is small incremental inventory, yet the downslide is a breakage causing a week of downtime and a massive inventory shortage, then the upside really isn't worth it. You may have experienced a time you got food poisoning at a restaurant. The downside is so bad, compared with the upside of "It's just a meal," that you never go back there again. On the other hand, if the upside is very significant, despite the downside being bad, you might take the chance. If the person of your dreams wanted to meet you at that very same restaurant that gave you food poisoning, you might consider the upside worth the potential downside. You agree to meet at the restaurant. The upside of buying a lottery ticket with a jackpot of $100 million is so great compared to the downside of losing $2 that you take the chance, however ill advised doing so is statistically.

5. *Ignoring the statistical downside:* Can you ignore the statistical downside *emotionally?* Take crossing the street; you might get hit by a car, but you still cross streets. If it's a four-lane highway, you might not be able to ignore the downside and won't cross. However, if it's a two-lane road with a stoplight, you wouldn't give it a second thought. In this case, you would ignore the statistical downside.

6. *Absorption capability:* How easy (or difficult) will it be to absorb (recover from) the downside if it were to occur? Let's say you have a customer who rarely purchases; when he does, it's a small amount. If

you decide to stop selling an item, you might lose him as a customer (downside). He is one of 1,500 customers, and his revenue is so small it wouldn't make much of a difference; you absorb the loss. On the other hand, if your best customer—someone who accounts for 25 percent of your revenue—cancelled, it would be a severe problem you could not absorb. You might have to reduce your staff or even go out of business.

7. *Controllability:* Do you have—or think you have—control over the situation? For example, you don't have much control related to the risk of a crash when flying in an airplane. However, you may have great control of the risk associated with a bad pricing decision. Despite the number of car accidents, most people think they are in control when driving. As many parents tell their newly licensed children, "I know you are a good driver, but you are not in total control, because there are other drivers who are not as cautious. So be careful!"

8. *Necessity of the upside:* How crucial is the decision's upside? Driving your car has risks, but if you live in the suburbs, you may need to drive to get to work or to stores. It may be necessary. The greater the need, the easier it is to ignore the statistical downside, because you simply must do something. There's a chance—however remote—that you might trip and break a bone merely walking from one room to another. You usually ignore that possibility, because you can't live your life in one place; you must move around.

9. *Reversibility:* Can you reverse the decision if a downside occurs? If you are a parachutist, the decision to leap out of an airplane is irreversible; you can't change your mind. However, if you decide to buy a new coat, you can usually return it within a specific period of time. *That* decision is completely reversible.

10. *Mitigation strategy:* This is about minimizing the impact if the downside occurs. Your mitigation strategy is your plan to react to issues that arise from the occurrence of the downside. Let's say you planned to drive to an important meeting, but your car breaks down. You might be able to take a taxi, borrow a friend's car, or get a ride. If you're in the software business and you discover a problem in your product, a mitigation strategy would be providing a patch for your customers to download that fixes the problem.

11. *Preeminent metrics:* A preeminent metric is a measurement to predict a downside far enough in advance that you can avoid the prediction coming true. For example, let's say you're tracking project progress with a metric related to percentage completed over time. One of the milestone deliverables looks like it might be delayed. You're tracking the progress far enough in advance that you can reallocate resources, compensate, and make up the delay. If you had not measured the progress this way, you would not have been able to compensate. We call the measurement a *preeminent metric* if it allows you to predict a bad outcome far enough in advance that you can change things and prevent that bad outcome from occurring.

Using the 11-Factor Model

Instead of asking, "What is the risk?" or "What is the downside?" critical thinking requires us to say, "Let's take a look at the risk factors to get clear on the risk." Here's an example of all the factors at work.

Let's say you're working on a new application suite to streamline communications between departments during a customer incident. This headscratcher's goal is to shorten response time while providing your customer with accurate information, as well as to increase the number of customers supported, because the current system is at maximum capacity. You've designed the process, tested it with the new applications, and concluded it's time to roll it out. You go to the steering committee, because it had asked to be notified when you were ready to go live and announce, "We are ready to implement the new process and systems." The committee will need to decide to go or no-go, so it asks about the risk in moving forward. You detail the following:

- *Downside:* The process was tested and will reduce time, but the downside is that the learning curve may take longer than expected, resulting temporarily in a slower response time. Also, if there is a failure in either the process or the new applications, the customer might get the wrong information.

- *Probability of the downside:* We did loads of testing, so the probability of the downside is reasonably low. We found that 15 of 100 cases took longer than the old process, but 85 were shorter. When testing for accurate responses, the new process produced inaccurate responses 7 percent of the time, in contrast to 15 percent of the time with the old process. However, if the learning curve for all those involved is slower than we anticipate or the new applications fails, we will most likely see a significant increase in our response time to customers—perhaps as high as 50 percent. Accuracy would decrease by about that amount as well.

- *Upside:* We're doing this to accommodate more customers and improve our quality of responses. This will have a significant effect on the success of our business.

- *Probability of the upside:* Overall, the probability of success is upward of 95 percent, thanks to all of the testing we did.

- *Ignoring the statistical downside:* Although downsides could occur, we have an excellent reputation with these kinds of changes. We also have a detailed mitigation plan in the event things go wrong. We make these kinds of changes several times a year; although complicated, they're routine.

- *Absorption capability:* If the downside occurs—customer response time is slower, or the applications fail—we will implement our mitigation strategy. Although we'll be embarrassed, an apology letter to our customers would be sufficient, because we have a very loyal customer base and can afford the hit to our service quality.

- *Controllability:* Our rollout strategy is to implement the new process with different customer groups and not all at once. This will allow us to throttle the rollout and observe the results. We have the training programs in place and subject matter experts (SMEs) are ready to help.

- *Necessity of the upside:* The forecast is for a 20 percent customer increase over the next 12 months. We cannot accommodate that with our current system. We have no choice but to implement this new process and application suite if we continue to add customers.

- *Reversibility:* Although we could not reverse the minimal public relations damage, we have a plan to abort the rollout and revert to the old system temporarily.

- *Mitigation strategy:* If the downside occurs, we will first understand whether it's the result of a learning curve or the failure of the applications. In the event of an application failure, we'll implement our plan to revert to the old system until we fix the application. If it's a learning curve issue, we'll add resources to offset that and slow down the rollout to allow more time for people to master everything. We'll also have SMEs fully trained and experienced with the new system floating around to assist anyone who needs help.

- *Preeminent metrics:* We are monitoring the cues closely and running statistics to compare times and accuracy with the old system. If anything starts to move in the wrong direction, we will notice before it becomes an uncontrollable issue. We're very confident in this early warning system, because we've used it successfully before.

Given the preceding risk analysis, the steering committee says, "The benefit (upside) is significant. Although there is some risk in proceeding, we are confident your understanding of that risk, as well as the actions you'll take to both prevent it and mitigate it, is well thought out." You have a go!

Now let's take something much more basic, something you probably don't even think about: the risk of breathing. After all, you can catch a cold, catch a disease, or have a bad allergic reaction.

- *Downside:* Have a severe allergic reaction, choke on something you breathe in, or catch a terminal disease.

- *Probability of the downside:* We catch colds and the flu often; sometimes something much more serious is also a possibility. You probably have a 1 in 3 chance of catching a cold or the flu during the year; serious diseases, much less so.

- *Upside:* Of course, the upside of breathing is that *you get to live.*

- *Probability of the upside:* Extremely high with every breath. However, you acknowledge that you will catch a cold or the flu by breathing. If you took 20 breaths per minute, then you would take about 10 million breaths in a year. If you catch two colds in a year, then the probability of that downside (a cold) would be two in 10 million—definitely worth the risk of each breath.

- *Ignoring the statistical downside:* We generally don't even think about what we are breathing in, until we go to our doctor for an annual checkup and everyone in the office is coughing and hacking—or if there is an H1N1 flu outbreak, and you're walking around an airport wondering where everyone has been.

- *Absorption capability:* You get well almost all the time after you get a cold or flu. You can absorb a few days out from work. It's not so easy if you're very elderly, weak from other ailments, or battling a serious disease. These factors could have a significant impact on your family and yourself.

- *Controllability:* You stay healthier, eat right, avoid people who are sick, change your seat on a bus if the person next to you is coughing, and keep your immune system in check. This helps minimize the chances of catching an illness.

- *Need:* You absolutely need to breathe and cannot exist without doing so. You can't consciously stop it for long, either! Although the risk factors exist, you will always decide breathing is a go. As a result, although the other factors might affect your behavior here and there, they won't stop you from breathing. The absolute necessity trumps all other factors.

- *Reversibility:* If you get sick, there is no redo. You can't get unsick; you can only heal (or not heal).

- *Mitigation:* As soon as you feel bad, you can take an antibiotic or antiviral.

- *Preeminent metrics:* You can take your temperature. This won't prevent you from getting sick but could be an early warning system to receive treatment quickly. You listen to the news to hear about flu outbreaks.

What Is Too Risky?

When a person claims that something is too risky, that person is labeling it as such based on *their personal measure*. He thinks the risk doesn't warrant the benefit of a yea decision, so he says nay. You need to understand how they evaluate the risk factors to gain insight into *why* it's too risky. One way to figure this out for yourself is to work through the factors on simple decisions, such as riding a bike, eating a huge piece of chocolate cake, quitting your job for another, or crossing a footbridge over a ravine. Understanding how you use these risk factors will provide you with baselines when you evaluate risk on real business problems. For example, the risk you evaluate for skydiving might be very high on some factors. If a business decision has comparable risk, then it's probably something to avoid. On the other hand, if skydiving ends up being low risk from your perspective, then something comparable will also have low risk for you in business.

Getting Started with *Risk*

Here are some ideas about using criteria and evaluating risk:

- *When you list criteria, risk will always be on that list:* The decision maker will evaluate risk for any significant decision, although he or she may not be able to articulate the reasons *why* he or she is uneasy about the risk. Go through the risk factors with the decision maker to discover where the uneasiness comes from so that you can address it.

- *Risk should always be discussed.* You should review risk even if you're working by yourself. Because it's more about substance than quantity, you need to address risk factors. Doing so allows you to understand where your emotional concerns are coming from.

- *Look at risk early.* Although the decision step may come after conclusions, don't wait until you detail every little thing after a conclusion before you at least glance at risk. You don't want to have your first risk discussion while in front of the decision maker for final approval.

The Takeaway

Your decision criteria will always include risk. By making a conscious effort to evaluate risk and its factors, you'll understand where you and others are uncomfortable. Now you have something to discuss.

Exercises for Risk

1. What is your risk for bungee jumping? Why would you take the risk, or why not? What about the risk in quitting your job before you find a new one?

2. Evaluate the risk of driving after having one drink. What about two? What about three? Four?

3. If you are currently working on a project that affects customers, evaluate the risk of releasing the results of this project to your customers.

4. Your boss gives you a new, large, complicated project. She asks you, "How long will this take?" After getting clear on the project and perhaps using some triangular thinking to estimate time, you say, "It will take me four months to complete this." Your boss says, "Oh, that's too long. We need it in three months." What's the risk in saying okay?

5. You're nearly finished with reading this book. What's the risk in implementing some of what you learned? (Hint: Virtually none, especially compared with the tremendous upside!)

34 Summary of Decisions

Taking Action

Deciding is the last step before executing your conclusion; it's the go or no-go. If a decision of go is made, people get to work and execution begins. A decision is made by identifying the decision maker (*who*), ensuring there's a *need* to make a decision, determining *when* it will be made and, most important, identifying the *criteria* because if met, it's a go. Risk is a key criterion involved in all of this.

We can make decisions quickly, because we've done almost all the work during the steps of clarity and conclusions. If you find yourself having difficulty in getting a decision made, one of the preceding factors isn't clear, or you haven't reached a definitive conclusion yet. Decisions are not "Should I buy the blue one or the red one?" They are "I've concluded to buy the red one; should I now buy it or not?" If you're still trying to figure out what to do, then go back to conclusions.

You may have heard of someone second-guessing a decision; you probably have done it yourself. This happens when you rethink a decision after you've made it and occurs most often when the criteria for the decision weren't well thought out. After making the decision, the decision maker thinks about it a little more and uncovers another criterion that brings to question the go or no-go call. You can avoid this by vetting and talking about the criteria.

Getting Started

Consider the following questions and advice when you're looking for a decision:

- Am I certain *who* the decision maker is?

- Does the decision maker know he or she is the decision maker?

- Can I articulate the business need to make a decision?

- What's the date that the decision *must* be made by? Look for reasons to make it a must, such as time dependence. If the decision to get on the train isn't made by the time the train leaves, then the no-action, no-go decision is automatically made.

- Avoid the no-decision decision. This is the automatic no-go, because an opportunity has come and gone and no action has been taken.

- The decision maker will have criteria he or she uses to evaluate the go or no-go. Help the decision maker write down what the criteria are.

- Practice reviewing the *risk* factors. See how you weigh these factors. When the decision maker begins to contemplate risk, you'll be prepared to have that conversation.

Are We Done Yet?

You're clear, you've reached a conclusion on how to solve your headscratcher, and now a decision has been made to move forward (go). If we define *done* as "critically thinking about a headscratcher from clarity through a decision," then yes—you are done. However, there are a few caveats to being done—sorry!

You made assumptions back in the conclusions phase. It would be wise while executing your solution to check periodically to ensure that those assumptions are still good ones. If they turn out to be invalid, then your conclusion might not be a good one, and you might need to revisit your subsequent decision to go. For example, you concluded to expand your business to additional states where you are licensed and your competition is not. Because it would take your competition five years to get a license, you'd enjoy a nice advantage for several years. You made the decision to go, and you've started negotiating lease agreements. However, you just read an announcement (observation) that your competition has been acquired. Its new parent company is already licensed in these new states and is excited to expand as well. This new information just invalidated your assumption and shook your confidence in your conclusion. The actions you decided on are no longer going to yield the benefits as promised by those who persuaded you. You slow the train and temporarily halt the project so that you can revisit the decision that you founded on a conclusion whose premise just became weak.

Decisions move the ball forward. Although there's no guarantee you'll never have to backtrack, critical thinking will maximize the probability that you'll make decisive, quality decisions that will yield successful results.

Critical Thinking
Summary and Suggestions

Critical Thinking Summary

Critical thinking is the process of getting clear on a headscratcher, concluding what to do about it, and deciding to take action. I've presented numerous tools and techniques to use within each of those steps throughout the book.

Everyone can use critical thinking. Although it may come more naturally to some than to others, everyone's problem-solving and decision-making results will improve by using the tools and following the steps detailed in the previous chapters. The most important step in critical thinking is to *begin*.

Like any newly learned skill, critical thinking takes practice. You can practice 5 to 10 minutes daily with something you do every day—send e-mails, check your to-do list, or figure out where you might go out or what to make for dinner. Start with one tool, and then add one at a time. There is no expectation that you—or anyone, for that matter—will use all these tools constantly. It's simply not necessary. You might expand and use many more tools on a huge and complicated headscratcher, but most of the time, just a few tools will go a long way.

A note to executives: You have the ability to lead and see to it that members of your organization use critical thinking. There's only one thing you must do to make that happen: you'll have to make it *necessary.* Insist that presentations include the thinking that went into the conclusion. Use critical thinking in your staff meetings. See to it that critical thinking steps are part of people's goals. Integrate critical thinking into your key processes. (Note: If people must follow a process, and critical thinking is a part of it, then it is necessary for them to use critical thinking.) Become a critical thinking organization. Your people's enhanced performance will be a game changer for you and your company.

A note to supervisors, managers, and directors: You can affect your organization the most by using critical thinking. Be a thinking coach for your reports, and ask *so what* once a day to get people to think. Use critical thinking for your own problem solving and decision making. Present your ideas to upper management, using critical thinking tools. Influence senior management with well-thought-out premises. Create innovative solutions with your team using critical thinking. Your leadership will grow and shine.

A note to individual contributors: Improving your own problem-solving and decision-making skills will result in improved performance. You'll be able to make better recommendations; you'll be more productive; and your quality of work will go up. Use critical thinking with your peers. Be clear with your manager, and ask why. Remember that you may need to educate your manager as to why you are asking why. Critical thinking will aid your career goal, whether it's to become a manager and leader, take on more responsibilities, or simply perform your job better.

Critical Thinking—Let's Begin

Start by emptying your bucket to get your head in the right place. Consider the following suggestions:

- *Suggestion 1:* Start critical thinking practice with inspection and writing e-mails. Not only is this easy and good practice, but there's also an important side advantage. Write your e-mail; then before you hit Send, ask, "Is what I'm about to send clear? Could the recipient misinterpret what I've written?" You'll reap three benefits from this. First, you'll find your e-mails are shorter, because clarity often takes fewer words. Second, your thoughts will be clearer and better organized. Third, and most important, your e-mails will be more easily understood, resulting in potentially huge productivity gains. What happens if you send an unclear e-mail to someone? The recipient will respond with a question, which you'll then have to answer. The result is three e-mails generated instead of one. Consider how many e-mails would be sent around if you copied five people on an unclear e-mail. Even worse, what happens if you send an unclear e-mail out, and instead of asking questions, people just start to do their own interpretations of your e-mail? Imagine the productivity gains from inspecting just three important e-mails a day.

- *Suggestion 2:* Continue using critical thinking on small tasks and headscratchers:

  ◆ E-mails: Use inspection; perhaps ask *why*.

  ◆ Meeting invites: Ask about *need* and *why* regarding meeting invitations.

  ◆ Requirements: Inspect requirements and ask *why* they are required. Why are they necessary?

  ◆ Priorities: When setting priorities, ask for *need* and *so what*.

- *Suggestion 3:* Record your responses. When you ask yourself *why*, *so what*, or about *need*, or while you *inspect*, write down your responses. Have you ever had an idea you thought was clear but was difficult to write down? You are forced to organize your thoughts clearly when you write things down.

- *Suggestion 4:* When you're looking for solutions, and you think you have a good idea, ask, "What assumptions am I making?" and "Why am I making those assumptions?"

- *Suggestion 5:* Avoid spending more than 2 hours in a critical thinking session, no matter how complex the headscratcher—simply because it's tiring to think this way. Also, let your brain do some work for you in the background. Do a little critical thinking, then go work out or go to sleep and resume the next morning. Things will be clearer, or at least you'll have more ideas about how to tackle the problem.

- *Suggestion 6:* If you have only 10 minutes to think critically, ask the following:
  - ◆ Am I clear on the situation?
  - ◆ What assumptions can I make, and what facts, observations, and experiences am I using for those assumptions?
  - ◆ When concluding, ask, "How did I get to that conclusion?"
  - ◆ What criteria will be used to decide go or no-go?

- *Suggestion 7:* If you can, think critically *with* someone else. Asking each other questions and listening to responses will stimulate new questions and ideas. You can think critically by yourself, so long as you are disciplined enough to answer the hard questions.

- *Suggestion 8:* One of the best ways to practice critical thinking is to be a thinking coach. As a thinking coach, you'll ask questions, listen to responses, and ask more questions. Remember those questions, and use them when you're the one who needs critical thinking.

- *Suggestion 9:* Before implementing critical thinking in your work, talk it over with your manager so that he or she knows why you are asking so many questions.

- *Suggestion 10:* Understand *your* need to think critically. As you learned in Chapter 8, "Need," if you want a problem solved, it is really beneficial to understand why a solution is necessary. It's the same for implementing critical thinking. It requires work, so if you don't have a *need* to think critically, why would you?

Why did you read this book? What motivated you to do so? Why do you want to improve your problem-solving and decision-making skills? Are you looking for more responsibility or to be a more effective leader? Understand *why;* then understand why it's *necessary.* It might be a personal goal, a company goal, or your manager's goal. Make a personal commitment to try some of these strategies. You'll like the result and want more.

The Takeaway

Thinking smarter is about using your brain more intelligently. Critical thinking is an enabling tool set for smarter problem solving, decision making, and creativity. It isn't hard, but critical thinking takes practice and discipline. Practice with the small stuff, and then apply it to headscratchers that matter.

ABOUT THE AUTHOR

In 2004, Michael Kallet founded HeadScratchers (www.headscratchers .com), a company focused on training critical thinking for problem solving, decision making, and creativity. Its mission is to help people become better headscratchers.

Before forming HeadScratchers, Mike was a technology and operations executive with 25 years of experience in leading teams that created numerous award-winning products and services spanning computer and communications technologies and markets.

He has a bachelor of science degree in physics from Worcester Polytechnic Institute.

INDEX